"One Day if I do go to heaven, I'll look around and say, 'It ain't bad, but it ain't San Francisco'"

Herb Caen

San Francisco History

Alton Pryor

Stagecoach Publishing
5360 Campcreek Loop
Roseville, Ca. 95747
stagecoach@surewest.net
www.stagecoachpublishing.com

Little Known Tales In San Francisco History

ISBN: 978-0-692-24478-4

Alton Pryor

Once I knew the City very well, spent my attic days there, while others were being a lost generation in Paris, I fledged in San Francisco, climbed its hills, slept in its parks, worked on its docks, marched and shouted in its revolts. It had been to me in the days of my poverty and it did not resent my temporary insolvency.

John Steinbeck

Table of Contents

Chapter 1

The 1906 Earthquake

Workers clean bricks that broke loose in the 1906 San Francisco earthquake.
(Photo by National Archives and Records)

At 5:12 a.m. on April 18, 1906 the massive earthquake shook San Francisco and other areas for miles around. The tremor lasted less than a minute, but its impact destroyed 500 city blocks of San Francisco.

Within 30 hours of the earthquake's first jolt, a firestorm decimated all of the familiar buildings of

San Francisco. Infernos swept through the city for three days.

The earthquake and its ensuing fires killed an estimated 3,000 people and left half of the city's 400,000 residents homeless. Survivors slept in tents in city parks and the Presidio. They stood in long lines for food and were required to do their own cooking in the street to minimize the threat of additional fires.

One eye witness described this devastating scene.

> *When the fire caught the Windsor Hotel at Fifth and Market Streets there were three men on the roof, and it was impossible to get them down. Rather than see the crazed men fall in with the roof and be roasted alive the military officer directed his men to shoot them, which they did in the presence of 5,000 people"*

Another eye witness related this story:

> *Of a sudden we found ourselves staggering and reeling. It was as if the earth was slipping gently from under our feet. Then came the sickening swaying of the earth that threw us flat upon our faces.*
>
> *We struggled in the street. We could not get on our feet. Then it seemed as though my head was split with the roar that crashed into my ears. Big*

buildings were crumbling as one might crush a biscuit in one's hand. Ahead of me a great cornice crushed a man as if he were a maggot—a laborer in overalls on his way to the Union Iron works with a dinner pail on his arm.

Still a third eye witness described the scene this way:

The most terrible thing I saw was the futile struggle of a policeman and others to rescue a man who was pinned down in burning wreckage. The helpless man watched it in silence till the fire began burning his feet. Then he screamed and begged to be killed. The policeman took his name and address and shot him through the head.

The earthquake impacted an area of 300,000 square miles along the San Andreas Fault. Its impact stretched from southern California to western Nevada and on up to southern Oregon.

There was a surface rupture that extended for 200 miles and sporadically, for another 80 miles.

Damage in San Francisco was estimated at $20 million. Water and sewer lines were destroyed, telephone and transportation lines were crippled and the streets were buckled.

There was another $235 to $500 million in 1906 dollars in property damage.

A businessman by the name of Jerome Clark witnessed the devastation.

In every direction from the ferry building flames were seething, and as I stood there, a five-story building half a block away fell with a crash, and the flames swept clear across Market Street and caught a new fireproof building recently erected. The streets in place had sunk three or four feet, in others great humps appeared four or five feet high. Street car tracks were bent and twisted out of shape. Electric wires lay in every direction.

Witnesses said that wagons with horses hitched to them, drivers and all, were lying in the streets, all dead, struck and killed by the falling bricks.

The Call Building, which appeared to be all right at first glance, had moved at the base two feet at one end, out onto the sidewalk. The entire interior was twisted out of shape.

Water was pumped from the Bay in an effort to quell the fires. Water mains were all broken and there was no supply for the firemen, leaving them helpless.

It became necessary to dynamite some of the buildings. Some of San Francisco's most beautiful structures that had survived the earthquake but not the fire were sent tumbling, blown apart by the dynamite charges.

A lodger at the Palace Hotel described his escape:

14

I had $600 in gold under my pillow. I awoke as I was thrown out of bed. Attempting to walk, the floor shook so that I fell. I grabbed my clothing and rushed down into the office, where dozens were already congregated. Suddenly the lights went out, and every one rushed for the door.

Outside I witnessed a sight I never want to see again. It was dawn and light. I looked up. The air was filled with falling stones. People around me were crushed to death on all sides.

All around the huge buildings were shaking and waving. Every moment there were reports like 100 cannons going off at one time. Then streams of fire would shoot out and other reports followed.

I met a Catholic priest and he said, "We must get to the ferry." He knew the way and we rushed down Market Street.

At places the streets had cracked and opened. Chasms extended in all directions. I saw a drove of cattle, wild with fright, rushing up Market Street. I crouched besides a swaying building.

As the cattle came nearer they disappeared. They seemed to drop into the earth. When the last had gone I went nearer and found they had indeed been precipitated into the earth, a wide fissure having swallowed them.

15

How I reached the ferry I cannot say. It was bedlam, pandemonium and hell rolled into one. There must have been 10,000 people trying to get on the boat.

Men and women fought like wildcats to push their way on board. Clothes were torn from the backs of the men and women and children indiscriminately.

Amadeo Peter Giannini

Congress responded to the disaster in several ways. The House and Senate Appropriations Committees enacted emergency appropriations for the city to pay for food, water, tents, blankets and medical supplies.

They also appropriated funds to reconstruct many of the public buildings that were damaged or destroyed.

Amadeo Peter Giannini rushed to his Bank of Italy in downtown San Francisco. He was unsure what he would find in the wake of the earthquake that shook him out of bed.

In a borrowed produce wagon, Giannini rushed to his bank, which he founded two years earlier. He and some employees emptied the bank's vault, loading two million dollars in gold, coins and securities onto the borrowed produce wagon.

Amadeo Giannini opened the first Bank of Italy in San Jose.

The banker concealed his rich wagonload of gold and coins with a layer of vegetables to throw off potential robbers.

Other San Francisco bankers elected to stay closed during the days following the earthquake, allowing them to sort out the damage.

Not Giannini. He placed wooden planks across two barrels on the docks near San Francisco's North Beach to serve as a desk. He opened for business to extend credit to small businesses and individuals in need of money to start over.

Nine days after the quake, a newspaper advertisement announced the location of his bank's operation. He became known as the son of immigrants who loaned money to immigrants when other bankers refused. His western banking empire created a system of branch banks to serve ordinary people.

His actions in 1906 are credited with spurring San Francisco's recovery following the tremor and the fire that ravaged the city.

A.P. Giannini was the son of Italian immigrants. He was born in San Jose in 1870. A disgruntled employee killed his father over a dollar debt when Amadeo was seven years of age.

His mother later married Lorenzo Scatena, a teamster who then entered the produce business. Giannini left school at age 14 to assist him. The business thrived, its success based on the impeccable reputation for integrity that Giannini exuded.

At age 31, he announced that he was selling his half-interest in the business to his employees and retiring. He once said, "I don't want to be rich. No man actually owns a fortune. It owns him."

Banks that maintained a policy of lending only to wealthy clients angered Giannini. He opened his Bank of Italy in a San Francisco saloon in 1904, determined to serve the little fellow.

Giannini had ample opportunity to live up to his philosophy when the 1906 earthquake shook the city to pieces. Giannini loaned customers money based on nothing but a signature.

When he opened his bank in 1904, he offered those potential customers that were ignored by other bankers the opportunity to open savings accounts and get loans.

Within a year, deposits with his Bank of Italy were soaring above $700,000 a hefty amount by current standards. He courted immigrants from the Yugoslavian, Russian, Mexican, Portuguese, Chinese, Greek and other communities. By the mid-1920s, he owned the third largest bank in the nation.

A major portion of the bank's first day deposits came from small tradesmen who had been actively solicited by Giannini and other members of the bank. Often, a depositor's ignorance of English or bank procedure required that the bank's personnel fill out deposit slips and checks.

Giannini viewed the earthquake as offering an opportunity for his Bank of Italy. His personal knowledge of his customers' accounts allowed him to resume operations quickly.

In less than six weeks following the earthquake, deposits in the Bank of Italy exceeded withdrawals.

When, in mid-1907 Giannini heard rumblings of a financial downturn despite the nation's apparent prosperity at the present time, he took action. He began increasing his bank's gold reserves, urged customers to increase their deposits while at the same time reducing their outstanding loans.

When the financial panic did hit, Giannini's bank was in position to tackle the financial collapse head-on. The Bank of Italy did not have to invoke rules limiting withdrawals or requiring advance notice before withdrawals as competing banks did.

Giannini's greatest accomplishment may have been the institution of branch banking. He studied the branch banking situation occurring in Canada. When California enacted a law in 1909 allowing branch banking, Giannini was already ahead of the game.

Directors of the Bank of Italy authorized opening such a bank in San Jose on Columbus Day, 1909. By 1918, the Bank of Italy became the first statewide branch banking system in the U.S., with 24 branches throughout California.

In the late 1920s, Giannini approached Orra E. Monnette, president and founder of the Los Angeles based Bank of America. The Los Angeles bank exhibited strong growth as a result of developing an advanced bank branching system

Giannini's Bank of Italy merged with Monnette's Bank of America in 1929. They used The Bank of America as the name of their joint operation, and Giannini and Monnette served as co-chairs of the new bank.

Giannini died in 1949 at age 79. By the time of his death, Bank of America was California's largest, the nation's largest, and the world's largest commercial and savings bank.

Chapter 2

Chinatown

Chinatown in San Francisco

San Francisco's Chinatown is the oldest Chinatown in North America and the largest Chinese community outside Asia.

It was established in 1848 and continues to retain its own customs, languages, places of worship, social clubs and identity.

Chinatown draws more visitors annually than does Golden Gate Park.

According to the San Francisco Planning Department, Chinatown is the most densely populated urban area west of Manhattan. It has

15,000 residents living within 20 square blocks. In 1970, the population density of Chinatown was seven times the San Francisco average.

When the ship "Eagle" docked in San Francisco in 1848, it carried the first Chinese immigrants to California, two men and a woman.

The two men went to work in the gold mines while the woman worked as a domestic for a family that had lived in China. These early immigrants led the way for the arrival of more than seven hundred Chinese in 1849.

By 1852, there were eighteen thousand Chinese men and only fourteen Chinese women in the state. This number would grow to 116,000 during the next fourteen years.

Some of the Chinese began working the abandoned placer mines of the Anglo miners, contenting themselves with less than half the return the original miners received. Their persistence and hard work brought about the wrath of the white miner population.

There were many who feared the industriousness of the Chinese immigrants, and it led to a great deal of prejudice in some quarters. These odd-appearing people from the Far East were considered "barbarians" who were encroaching on American territory.

One lawmaker introduced a measure that would have confined the Chinese to jobs as apprentices, but without success.

This didn't stop lawmakers from trying again, in 1854, to impose a tax on any Asian landing in California.

Lee's Meats in San Francisco's Chinatown

The tax, which was established at $50 per head, was struck down by the state supreme court as unconstitutional.

Undaunted, the California legislature then imposed, in 1854, a foreign miners' tax of six dollars a month. This tax was soon raised to eight dollars, and then again to ten dollars.

Legislators then enacted a law that excluded the testimony of a person of Chinese descent from testifying in any court case involving an Anglo.

The Chinese situation presented Californians with a dilemma. If the Asians were driven from the mines, it would mean a loss of thousands of dollars in miners' taxes. To leave them in the mines meant, assuredly, an increase in racial violence.

There was fear, too, that driving them from the mines would cause stress in other areas. For instance, the Chinese would leave the mines only to go into towns and agricultural districts where they would work for the barest wage, undercutting other workmen.

In exasperation, state law-makers, in 1858, passed a law forbidding any more Chinese being brought into California. If a ship's captain were convicted of disobeying this order, he would be liable to a fine of $400 to $600 dollars, or imprisonment for up to one year.

A catch-all tax was enacted in 1862. This was a police tax amounting to $2.50 a month, which was to be levied on any Chinese male eighteen years of age or older not subject to the miners' tax.

The Supreme Court declared this tax unconstitutional. The court did uphold the law excluding Chinese testimony in court as legal, however.

So hostile was the racial environment in the 1860s that students of Chinese, Blacks or Indians could be barred from public schools. The law did allow for separate schools to be provided.

This law was modified in 1866 to read that Chinese students could be admitted to schools, if there were no objections by white parents.

Chinese immigrants provided important labor for a number of industries in the building of California, not the least of which was the railroads. Charles Crocker's construction boss for the Central Pacific scoured the state for Chinese workers.

The need for more railroad workers resulted in the Pacific Mail Steamship Line bringing more workers directly from China. At one time, there was an estimated ten thousand to fifteen thousand Chinese laborers working on the railroad in California.

When the railroad was finished, Chinese laborers inundated San Francisco in 1870, flooding the labor market there. They were willing to work at any job for virtually any pay.

Again, the eager legislature stepped in and passed a law that would provide a fine of $1,000 to $5,000 on anyone bringing Chinese or Japanese nationals into California who could not provide evidence of the person's good character. This law, too, was declared unconstitutional.

The court's ruling did not deter the city council of San Francisco, however. This body passed an ordinance that prohibited any Chinese or Japanese from working on municipal public works.

Other counties joined the fray. Irrigation companies, by 1876, were expressly forbidden to use any Chinese workers on projects in Alameda, Contra Costa, San Jose, Stanislaus, Merced, Fresno, and Tulare counties.

There were many other instances of abuse against the Chinese population. San Francisco enacted a city rental ordinance calling for a fine of ten to fifty dollars per person if a space of less than five hundred feet per occupant was not available. The law was upheld in court.

Another ordinance required any male Chinese prisoner convicted of crimes in the city to have his hair cut within one inch of his head. This was said to be a greater indignity for the Chinese male than having his ears cropped. The mayor mercifully vetoed the law as being unnecessary and barbarous.

In San Francisco during the 19th century, the Chinese population was predominantly male because U.S. policies made it difficult for Chinese women to enter.

Chinatown was the one geographical region deeded by the city government that allowed

Chinese persons to inherit and inhabit dwellings within the city.

During the California Gold Rush, one of the most successful Chinese in San Francisco was Ah Toy.

Ah Toy arrived in San Francisco from Hong Kong in 1849. She was a tall attractive woman with bound feet.

When she left China, she traveled with her husband, who died during the voyage. She spent little time mourning his loss. She soon became the mistress of the ship's captain.

The captain showered her with gold to the point that when she reached San Francisco she had a bit of money. Ah Toy noticed the lusty looks she received from the miners in San Francisco.

She figured they would pay for a closer peep. She opened her own peep show which proved successful. In 1850, she opened a chain of brothels at 34 and 36 Waverly Place in Chinatown.

Ah Toy imported girls from China as young as eleven years old to work for her.

From 1868 to 1928, Ah Toy lived a quiet life in Santa Clara County. She died three months short of her one hundredth birthday.

Anti immigrant sentiment became law as the United States government passed the Chinese Exclusion Act of 1882—the first immigration restriction law aimed at a single ethnic group.

This law, along with other immigration restriction laws greatly reduced the numbers of Chinese allowed into the U.S. Immigration was effectively limited to immigration of single males only.

The Chinese Exclusion Act was repealed during World War II in recognition of China as an ally in the war.

From the mid 1870s, Tong wars sprang up over turf battles concerning criminal enterprises. During the 1880s and 1890s, roughly 20 to 30 tongs ran highly profitable gambling houses, brothels, opium dens and slave trade enterprises in Chinatown.

When San Francisco's 1906 earthquake destroyed Chinatown's wooden tenements, it also dealt a death blow to the powerful tongs.

In March 1990, a Chinese-born man who was a long-time resident of Chinatown, was found dead with bubonic plague. The next morning, all of Chinatown was quarantined.

Police stopped all people of Asian heritage from leaving or entering Chinatown as the San Francisco Board of Health looked for more cases. The health department started burning personal property and sanitizing buildings, streets and sewers in Chinatown.

Chinese Americans protested, and the Chinese Consolidated Benevolent Association threatened lawsuits. The quarantine was lifted but the burning and fumigating continued.

A federal lawsuit was decided against the right of the health department to close off Chinatown without any proof that Chinese Americans were more susceptible to plague than Anglo Americans.

The four-year death toll from the plague was 113 people, almost all from a ten-block area of Chinatown.

Chapter 3

The Magnificent Bridges

S an Francisco is as well-known for its suspension bridges as it is for its buildings and other architecture.

The San Francisco Bay toll bridge was conceived in the Gold Rush days, but construction didn't didn't begin until 1933. It opened for traffic in 1936, six months before its sister bridge, The Golden Gate Bridge.

The Bay Bridge first carried automobile traffic on its upper deck and trucks and trains on its lower level.

Being located at the mouth of San Francisco Bay, the city was in a perfect location to prosper during the California Gold Rush. Almost all goods not produced locally arrived by ship.

When the first transcontinental railroad was built, San Francisco was on the wrong side of the bay to benefit from the rail line. The Bay Bridge was long under consideration.

Support for a trans-bay crossing grew in the 1920s with the increasing popularity and availability of the automobile. In 1929, the California legislature established the California Toll Bridge Authority.

The purpose was to build a bridge to connect San Francisco with Alameda County by way of a bridge.

In like fashion, the Golden Gate Bridge was conceived to connect San Francisco with Marin County, bridging both U.S. 101 and California State Route 1 across the three-mile strait.

The Golden Gate Bridge opened in 1937 and was at 4,200 feet, the longest suspension bridge main span in the world until 1964.

Prior to the opening of the Golden Gate Bridge, the Sausalito Land and Ferry Company service was the largest ferry service in the world. It was a subsidiary of the Southern Pacific Railroad.

The ferry crossing between the Hyde Street Pier in San Francisco and to Sausalito in Marin County took about 20 minutes and cost $1 per vehicle.

The Golden Gate Bridge

Before the Golden Gate Bridge was built, San Francisco was the largest American city still served primarily by ferry boats.

Many experts said a bridge couldn't be built across the 6,700 foot strait. It had strong swirling tides and currents, with water 372 feet deep at the center of the channel. The naysayers claimed frequent and ferocious winds and blinding fogs would prevent construction.

A movable safety netting installed beneath the construction saved the lives of many otherwise unprotected steel workers. Eleven men were killed during construction of the bridge.

Ten of these were killed when the bridge was near completion and the net failed under the stress of a scaffold which had fallen.

Nineteen others who were saved by the net during construction became proud members of the "Half Way to Hell Club".

San Francisco's skyline can be seen from the Bay Bridge photo.

The San Francisco Bay Bridge cost $77 million. In 1989 the Loma Prieta earthquake caused a 50-foot section of the bridge to collapse.

The unofficial name for the Bay Bridge is "The James 'Sunny Jim' Rolph Bridge". The name has rarely been use and was not recognized until the bridge's 50th anniversary. James Rolph was a mayor of San Francisco from 1912 to 1931.

When the Bay Bridge opened in 1936, the toll was 65 cents, and collected in each direction. Within months, the toll was reduced to 50 cents in order to compete with the ferry system. The toll was lowered again to 25 cents when it was realized that this amount was sufficient to pay off the original revenue bonds.

When the bridge was being planned, San Francisco city engineer Michael O'Shaughnessy figured it would cost up to $100 million. He sought lesser bids from various engineers. Joseph Strauss, a five-foot tall engineer from Chicago designed a bridge that could be built for $17 million.

Using advances in metallurgy and bridge design, Strauss abandoned his original concept and replaced it with a pure suspension bridge.

Chapter 4

Emperor Norton

Emperor Norton

Joshua Abraham Norton was a picturesque figure and the citizens of San Francisco adopted and gave him the royal treatment he demanded. Norton, you see, proclaimed himself

Norton I, Emperor of the United States and Protector of Mexico.

The peculiar Norton was one of California's most colorful figures, although few history books mention him. Little is known about him. He was born about 1818 in London, England, but grew up in South Africa where his parents went to seek their fortune.

"The Emperor further orders that anyone posting this defamatory picture of himself with the two vile curs known as Bummer and Lazarus shall add the following disclaimer: 'These are not the Emperor's dogs'".

In 1849, Norton sailed to San Francisco aboard the Dutch Schooner Franzika, enticed by reports that gold lay there simply for the taking. He carried a nest egg of $30,000 with which he opened a business selling supplies to gold miners.

At the same time, he invested in land that was called San Francisco's Cow Hollow district.

Norton was considered one of San Francisco's most respected businessmen. He rebounded from the big fire of 1853 and diversified his operations. Already his friends were referring to him as *"Emperor"*. Norton was so successful that he was invited to become a member of the elite San Francisco Vigilance Committee.

Norton then conceived the bold idea of cornering the San Francisco rice market. The large Chinese population would provide a captive and hungry market for his rice. The only rice available was imported aboard cargo steamships.

Because of his previous investment successes, he soon signed on a number of ready investors. It was only a matter of days until he owned, practically speaking, all of the rice in San Francisco.

His downfall came when two ships arrived through the Golden Gate, both loaded with rice. While Norton had the money to buy one of the shipments, he could not afford to buy two such shipments. This meant he no longer held a corner on San Francisco's rice market.

With this glut of rice hitting the town, Norton was financially ruined. During the next three years, he spent most of his time in court, and emerged penniless in 1858.

Norton packed his meager belongings and disappeared from San Francisco for about nine months. There are no records of his whereabouts during the period he was gone.

Suddenly, in the late summer of 1859, Norton returned to San Francisco, walking proudly through the streets in a beaver hat and naval regalia. He was arguably mad, for soon after his return, he walked into the offices of the San Francisco Bulletin and presented them with this single sentence, which they ran in the next edition's front page:

"At the peremptory request of a large majority of the citizens of these United States, I, Joshua Norton, formerly of Algoa Bay, Cape of Good Hope, and now for the past nine years and ten months of San Francisco, California, declare and proclaim myself Emperor of these U.S., and in virtue of the authority thereby in me vested do hereby order and direct the representatives of the different States of the Union to assemble in Musical Hall of this city, on the 1st day of February next, then and there to make such alterations in the existing laws of the Union as may ameliorate the evils under which the country is laboring, and thereby cause confidence to exist, both at home and abroad, in our stability and integrity."

Norton I
Emperor of the United States
September 17, 1859

The populace loved him. When the people read his proclamation in the Bulletin, they began greeting him with deep bows and curtsies. In return, one writer said, "San Francisco has a wise and caring monarch to reign over its gilded cage."

The self-proclaimed emperor ruled his new domain by proclamation. It didn't faze him that not all of his edicts were carried out. If taxes or water rates were too high, he simply commanded that they be lowered. If there were inadequacies in city services, he ordered improvements.

He was also involved in national issues. On the eve of the Civil War, he temporarily dissolved the Union, and after the Prussian victory in 1872, he ordered a week of continuous celebration and thanksgiving.

Bay area newspapers were delighted and competed for the honor of printing his proclamations. Some accused newspapers of creating fake proclamations to stimulate reader interest, a practice against which the Emperor railed angrily.

Emperor Norton attended every public function or meeting, always arriving on foot or bicycle rather than coach, and performed daily rounds of his city's streets, making sure that police were on their beats and that cleanliness, harmony and order prevailed.

He was quick to anoint those that did good deeds. If he noticed someone performing a kind act, he might spontaneously ennoble him or her. The titles were especially popular with children, who would follow him in groups, looking everywhere for litter to pick up or old ladies to help across the street.

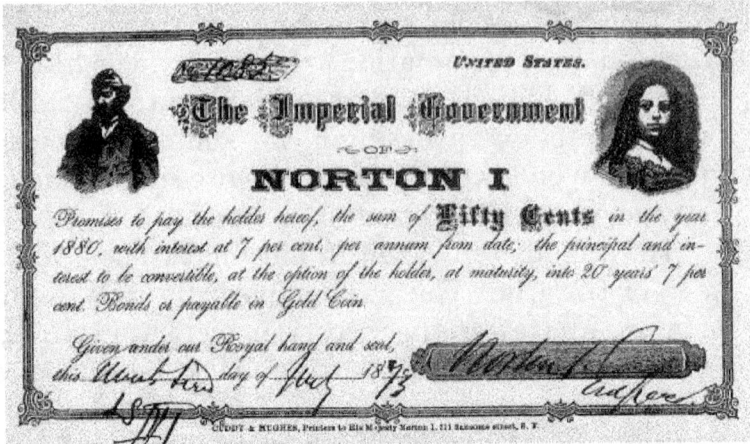

When Emperor Norton needed money, he simply issued his own script, such as the 50-cent bill above.

Norton's enchantment with San Francisco was returned in kind by San Francisco merchants and the public. His expenses were few. He could eat free at whatever restaurant suited his particular taste that day. He had three seats reserved for him at every theatrical performance (one for himself and one each for his famously well-behaved dogs, Bummer and Lazarus).

Author's note: There are some who say that Bummer and Lazarus were simply stray dogs and did not belong to Norton at all)

The city paid for Norton's majestic uniforms and the local Masonic Lodge paid for his small apartment. He paid the 50 cents a day lodging out of his receipts from begging.

If he needed cash, that was no problem. Norton simply printed his own currency. His cash was accepted without question. He didn't hesitate to levy imperial assessments on business owners. His normal procedure was to walk into the offices of an old business friend and politely announce an assessment of ten million or so dollars. The business owner could quickly talk him down to two or three, or perhaps a cigar, with which he would walk out completely satisfied.

San Francisco's police did not quite know how to handle the self-proclaimed emperor. In January of 1867, he was arrested by an over-zealous rookie policeman with the order that he "be confined for treatment of a mental disorder," and held at the police station pending a hearing.

The public was outraged. Every newspaper editorial denounced the action, and it was feared a riot would ensue. Police Chief Patrick Crowley himself opened the cell doors, and issued a lengthy public apology to the Emperor.

Norton was magnanimous about the whole affair and his relations with the police became much more congenial. He would lead their annual parades and inspect new cadets. These members of what he called his Imperial Constabulary saluted him when he passed.

There were some who believed Norton's madness was all an act, that one day he had decided to pull a prank, and because of the gullibility of the populace, got away with it for years.

Some felt that Emperor Norton's proclamations betrayed a complex, analytical man (though still mad). Samuel Clemens (Mark Twain), then a San Francisco newspaperman working next door to Norton's flophouse, saw Norton virtually every day.

Clemens hated those who belittled the self-styled emperor, especially newspaper columnist Arthur Evans, who wrote under the pseudonym of "Colonel Mustard".

Years later, Clemens revealed that he had based the character of the King in *Huckleberry Finn* on the eccentric Joshua Norton. In his book the *"Prince and the Pauper"*, a story of confused identities, Twain paid homage to Norton.

As emperor, Norton frequently sent cables to fellow rulers, offering surprisingly well informed advice. While many of the responses he got back were forgeries devised by his friends to make him happy, many were not.

King Kamehameha of Hawaii was so taken with the Emperor's insight and understanding that towards the end of his life he refused to recognize the U.S. State Department, saying instead he would deal only with representatives of the Empire.

Despite the fact that Norton was perceived to be mad, some of his proclamations became reality. For instance, he had issued numerous proclamations proposing and then finally commanding the construction of a suspension bridge linking San Francisco and Oakland.

He provided his own design sketches. His planned terminus is within a block of where the Bay Bridge ends now. A plaque there is said to bear testimony of the emperor's foresight.

Norton I died quite suddenly of apoplexy on January 8, 1880, on the corner of California and

Grant. He left no heirs. San Francisco mourned his passing. Ten thousand people, from all walks of life, lined up to view his remains. His funeral cortege was two miles long.

Emperor Norton began his Imperial Reign in San Francisco with this proclamation!

Proclamation I

At the preemptory request and desire of a large majority of the citizens of these United States, I, Joshua Norton, formerly of Algoa Bay, Cape of Good Hope, and now for the last 9 years and 10 months past of San Francisco, California, declare and proclaim myself Emperor of these U.S., and direct the representatives of the different States of the Union to assemble in Musical Hall, of this city, on the 1st day of February next, then and there to make such alterations in the existing laws of the union as may ameliorate the evils under which the country is laboring, and thereby cause confidence to exist, both at home and abroad, in our stability and integrity.

Norton I
Emperor of the United States
17th September 1859

At 2:39 p.m. that day, during his funeral, San Francisco experienced a total eclipse of the sun. Fifty-four years later, Norton's coffin was reinterred at Woodlawn Cemetery in Colma. Flags throughout the city were lowered and businesses closed their doors. An estimated 60,000 people attended the ceremony, which was accompanied by full military honors.

When Emperor Norton heard of an East Coast pretender to his throne, he issued the following denunciation.

Proclamation II

Down with usurpers and imposters! Off with his head! So much for cooking other people's geese! The legitimate authorities of New York are hereby commanded to seize upon the person of one Stellifer, styling himself King or Prince of the House of David, and send him in chains to San Francisco, California, for trial before our Imperial Court, on various charges of fraud alleged again him in the public prints.

Norton I
Emperor of the United States
and Protector of Mexico
San Francisco 6th day of November 1865

Emperor Norton was indeed ahead of his time with this proclamation.

Proclamation III

Whereas, it is our pleasure to acquiesce in all means of civilization and population:

I Norton I, Emperor of the United States and protector of Mexico, do order and direct first, that Oakland shall be the coast termination of the Central Pacific Railroad; secondly, that a suspension bridge be constructed from the improvements lately ordered by our royal decree at Oakland Point to Yerba Buena, from thence to the mountain range of Saucileto (sic), and from thence to the Farallones, to be of sufficient strength and size for a railroad; and thirdly, te Central Pacific Railroad Company are charged with the carrying out of this work, for purposes that will hereafter appear. Whereof fail not under pain of death. Given under our hand this 18th day of August, A.D. 1869.

Norton I

The Emperor was just warming up. The newspapers loved to print his proclamations and edicts.

Proclamation IV

Whereas a war vessel belonging to our friend the emperor of Japan is on a visit and is at present in our harbor; and whereas, we are desirous of being courteous to strangers; now, therefore, we, Norton I, Dei gratia emperor, do hereby command all persons to show the officers and crew every attention, so that commerce may be benefitted thereby.

Norton I

Given under our royal hand and seal this 23d December, 1875.

Norton's 5th missive concerns funds he expected to receive.

Proclamation V

The following telegram has been received by His Imperial Majesty Norton I:

Dear Brother—It is with extreme regret that I receive yours announcing the non-arrival of the $14,000,000 which I forwarded sometime since. Be assured that the matter will be immediately looked into, and no stone left unturned looking to the receiving and safe delivery to you of the coin.

Hoi Tang, Emperor

The emperor commands the persons who are in possession of this money to forthwith give up its possession of the coin under penalty of our supreme displeasure.

Norton I

The emperor was not yet done. He issued the following edict in 1879.

Proclamation VI

Whoever after due and proper warning shall be heard to utter the abominable word "Frisco", which has no linguistic or other warrant, shall be deemed guilty of a High Misdemeanor, and shall pay into the Imperial Treasury as penalty the sum of twenty-five dollars.

The Emperor has even more to say. Let's hear him out.

Proclamation VI

Whoever after due and proper warning shall be heard to utter the abominable word "Frisco", which has no linguistic or other warrant, shall be deemed guilty of a High Misdemeanor, and shall pay into the Imperial Treasury as penalty the sum of twenty-five dollars.

Chapter 5

Founders of
San Francisco
(Was it Richardson or De Anza?)

William A. Richardson, founder of San Francisco.
(Google Images)

William A. Richardson was born in London, England. He deserted an English whaler when it put into San Francisco in 1822. He was tall, fair-haired, blue-eyed and only 27 years old.

Richardson petitioned Spanish Governor Pablo Vicente Sola for permission to stay in California.

Permission was granted on one condition. Richardson must teach the neophytes at Mission Dolores how to construct small boats for use in the bay.

Mission Delores

He taught carpentry, boatbuilding and navigation at the Mission. He also began building the first house of any substance in San Francisco. He planned to use the residence as a trading post.

He engaged in trading hides and tallow, and transported these supplies out of the Bay in small boats to the ocean-going ships that lay outside. At that time, none of the regular ocean-going liners came into the Bay.

He sold the pelts of otters to Boston traders for $40 to $60 each. Otters were plentiful in the bays and rivers of California.

Captain Richardson would later have the distinction of piloting the first deep-sea ship to enter San Francisco Bay, landing it in Sausalito.

At that early date, the only European communities were those located in the Presidio and the Mission. The European community consisted of Spanish soldiers and Spanish missionaries.

True Story of How San Francisco Got Its Name

San Francisco—this a derivative word from sand and Francisco. In the early settlement of this country it was the custom of an old monk of the interior, by the name of Jeremiah Francisco, to perform a pilgrimage to this place every month to visit the tomb of his brother whose remains he had here interred.

The wind "blew like mad", and upon his return he was usually so covered with the dust and sand, that his neighbors were unable to recognize him; hence they soon began to call him sand Francisco.

On one of his pilgrimages he happened, by mistake, to die here, and the place ever after was called by his name. From the difficulty of enunciating the "d", it was usually called "SAN" FRANCISCO, and has so continued to this day. The present popular notion that the place was named after the St. Francis Hotel is in error!

In 1823, Richardson converted to Catholicism. He became a naturalized citizen of Mexico, changed his name to Guillermo Antonio Richardson, and married a Mexican.

He took as his bride the daughter of Lieutenant Ygnacio Martinez, the Commandante of the Presidio.

Richardson acquired large tracts of land in Marin County, where he raised horses and cattle. He also owned two blocks now incorporated in the Presidio.

He built the first house in San Francisco. It was a large piece of canvas stretched on four posts and covered by an old ship sail. The house was located at what is now 823-827 Grant Avenue, near Clay Street. Two years later, he built a more substantial structure of adobe bricks.

Richardson had charge of several schooners belonging to Mission Dolores and one belonging to Mission Santa Clara.

One of his enterprises was operating a barge from Sausalito to San Francisco, carrying fresh water for the city.

When, in 1835, Governor Jose Figueroa made Yerba Buena (Now San Francisco) California's second port of entry, Richardson was offered the position of Port Captain.

In 1845, Richardson received a land grant covering a vast territory. He called this place *Albion* after his English homeland.

He built a saw mill on a river's estuary, powered by a tide-driven water wheel. The clever design allowed the mill to operate whenever the tide was changing. Immense waves destroyed the mill in 1853.

Richardson lost the land grant in 1854 because the U.S. Land Commission never recognized his ownership.

While Richardson was instrumental in San Francisco's early development, it was Juan Bautista de Anza who first arrived at the future site of San Francisco with 247 colonists.

In 1772 De Anza made his first exploratory mission to the Pacific Coast. He established the first successful overland connections between the Mexican State of Sonora and northern California.

The Mexican viceroy was impressed with de Anza's accomplishment and commissioned him to establish a settlement along the Pacific Coast at San Francisco Bay.

On the fifteenth of December, 1774, Viceroy Bucarelli sent the following letter to Father Junipero Serra at Monterey:

> *In consideration that the port of San Francisco, when occupied, might serve as a base of subsequent projects, I have resolved that the founding of a fort shall take place by assigning twenty-eight men under a lieutenant and a sergeant.*
>
> *As soon as they are in possession of the territory, they will be sure proof of*

the king's dominion. For this purpose,
Captain Juan Bautista de Anza will
take a second exposition overland to
Monterey from Sonora (Mexico), where
he must recruit the said troops.

He will see that they take their
wives and children along so that they
may become attached to their domicile.

He will also bring sufficient
supplies of grain and flour, besides
cattle.

When the territory has been
examined, and the presidio is
established, it will be necessary to erect
the proposed missions in its immediate
vicinity.

Seagoing explorers, including Juan Rodriguez
Cabrillo, sailed along the northern coast of
California during the 16th and 17th centuries. The
natural harbor of San Francisco Bay eluded them.

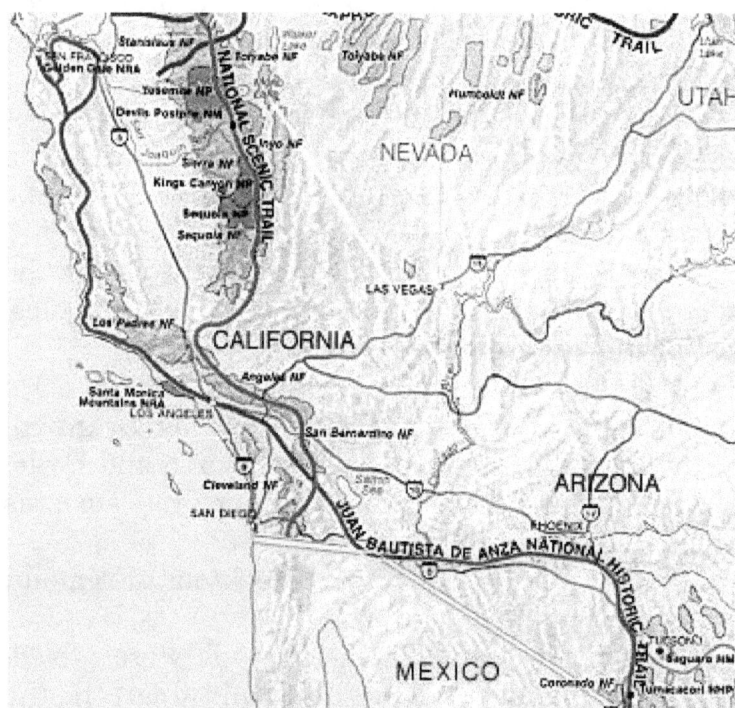

Juan Bautista De Anza National Trail

De Anza and his 247 colonists landed at the future site of San Francisco on March 28, 1776. He established a presidio, or military fort, on the tip of the San Francisco peninsula.

San Francisco remained an isolated and forgotten settlement for more than half a century.

When the U.S. took possession of California in 1848, San Francisco was still only a small town of 900 people. By 1852, after gold was discovered, it had grown to 36,000 residents.

According to *California, A Snapshot in Time*, by Janice Marshner, the first alcalde of San Francisco was *Don* Francisco de Haro. He commissioned artist Jean-Jacques Vioget to map out streets for the growing town in 1839.

Vioget created the grid pattern north of Market by mapping out the eight-block area between Montgomery, Sacramento, Grant and Pacific Streets.

In 1847, Jasper O'Farrell surveyed lots for the city so that they could be sold to raise revenues. Most of the lots were sold by 1849.

O'Farrell was the first to name any streets. He named them after townspeople such as Brannan, Bryant, Howard, Harrison, Leavenworth and Hyde. He also named some after Californians such as Vallejo, Larkin and Sutter.

Others include Kearny, Stockton, Fremont, Montgomery, and Taylor.

In 1850, few San Francisco roads were paved. They were muddy in the winter and dusty in the summer, and always cluttered with litter and by cargo because of a shortage of warehouses.

San Francisco's county government was established April 1, 1850. By the end of the year, many of the streets in the business district were graded and planked.

According to Marshner, in 1850 few of the buildings were personal residences. Prefabricated houses were imported to fill the void left when most of the carpenters left for the gold fields.

Hotels were expensive but not because they were luxurious. Most of them were makeshift lodging, built from plank and canvas. Guests provided their own bedding.

The St. Francis Hotel was the only hotel in town that provided sheets on its beds.

A treeless plaza located between Kearny, Washington, Grant and Clay streets was the social center of the city. It supported a flag staff and a platform for public speaking.

Located in the plaza was a store that sold stationery, newspapers and books (8,000 volumes). It also held a post office.

Long queues of people seeking word from home formed several lines at the post office every two weeks on "Steamer Day".

San Francisco's first mayor, John White Geary, set aside Union Square in the heart of San Francisco, for public use in 1850. It didn't take on the Union Square name until 10 years later when pro-union meetings were held there.

Chapter 6

Alcatraz
Island of the Pelicans

No better fortress could be devised to house prisoners than was the barren rock called Alcatraz. (Google Images)

W hen Spanish explorer Juan Manuel de Ayala first mapped the tiny speck of an island, he called it *La Isla de los Alcatraces.* Translated it means Island of the Pelicans.

That is how Alcatraz got its name in the year 1775. It lay barren for the next seventy-two years, when in 1847 the United States Army recognized the strategic value of the "Rock" as a military fortification.

A series of tunnels has been found underneath Alcatraz.

In 1853, the U.S. Army began building a military fortification on the island. Included in the construction was the Pacific Coast's first operating lighthouse.

The fortress on Alcatraz became a symbol of United State's military strength. The fortress was equipped with long-range iron cannons and four massive 36,000 pound 15-inch Rodman guns. Each of these guns could sink a hostile ship three miles away.

It was ironic that the island failed to live up to its reputation for firepower. It had only one occasion to fire one 400-pound cannon round at an unidentified ship. The shot missed its target by a wide margin.

Native Americans shunned Alcatraz, calling it "Evil Island". They believed the island was cursed.

The earliest recorded owner of the island of Alcatraz is Julian Workman, who was granted the property by Mexican Governor Pio Pico in June 1846. Workman was given the island with the understanding he would build a lighthouse on it.

In 1846, John C. Fremont bought the island in the name of the United States Government for $5,000. In 1850, President Ulysses S. Grant ordered that Alcatraz Island be set aside specifically as a U.S. Government military reservation.

Fremont expected a large compensation for his initiative for purchasing and securing Alcatraz for the U.S. The government invalidated the sale and paid Fremont nothing.

The U.S. Army found that Alcatraz was ideal as a long-term prison. The island was isolated and surrounded by frigid waters with hazardous currents.

Alcatraz gained a reputation for being a tough detention facility. Prisoners were separated into three groups based on their conduct and the crimes they had committed.

Prisoners in third class, for instance, were not allowed to have reading material from the library or visits and letters from relatives. A strict rule of silence was enforced at all time.

The Army, citing high operational costs, closed the prison in 1934. Ownership of the facility went to the Department of Justice.

The Great Depression ushered in a crime wave that aroused the public. People watched in fear as mobsters exerted their influence on metropolitan cities. Ill-equipped law enforcement agencies likewise cowered before the onslaught of organized crime and its mobsters.

The public's outcry to end the mayhem, brought renewed attention to Alcatraz, considered the ideal lodging place to house this new criminal element. It would not only serve as a housing facility for miscreants, but it would stand as a warning for those with criminal intent.

Special tear gas canisters were installed in the ceiling of the dining hall. Guards at various observation points could activate the canisters.

James A. Johnston was appointed warden. His background in business and his twelve years in the Department of Corrections served him well. He was also warden at San Quentin in 1913 and served briefly at Folsom prison.

Johnston had a strong interest in prisoner reform. He didn't believe in chain gangs.

Instead, he thought prisoners should report to a job where they would be respected and rewarded for their efforts.

In 1934, Alcatraz received a renovation. Electricity was run to each cell, and the walls of utility tunnels were cemented to insure that no criminal could enter or hide in them.

None of the 600 cells in the refurbished prison adjoined any perimeter wall. If an inmate did manage to tunnel through the cell wall, he would still need to find a way to escape from the cell house.

George "Machine Gun" Kelly was one of Alcatraz' most notorious prisoners.

Under Johnston, each prisoner was assigned his own cell. He received only basic necessities, which included food, water, clothing and medical care.

The prisoner's contact with the outside world was severed. Prison routine was rigid and unrelenting. As quickly as a given privilege was earned for good behavior, it could be taken away for the slightest infraction.

Warden Johnston met most of the new inmates assigned to Alcatraz. When he saw Al Capone in the lineup, Capone was grinning and making smug comments to other inmates.

When it came his turn to approach Johnston, he tried to show off to the other inmates by asking questions on their behalf. The warden handed him his prison number and ordered him back in line.

Capone made several attempts to con the warden out of special privileges, as he had done while incarcerated at the federal prison in Atlanta. The warden rejected all his attempts outright.

Capone finally admitted, "It looks like Alcatraz has got me licked."

Inmates rose at 6:30 a.m., and were allowed twenty-five minutes to tidy their cells and be counted. At 6:55 a.m., they were marched to the mess hall. They had twenty minutes to eat before going to their work assignments.

During its twenty-nine years of operation as a prison, there were fourteen attempted escapes, involving thirty-four inmates. Almost all of the escapees were either recaptured or killed.

Today, Alcatraz is an ecological preserve. It is also home to one of the largest gull colonies on the California coast.

Cellblocks at Alcatraz were stark and cold. Prisoners released from Alcatraz were not likely to want to return.   (Google Images)

The prison costs $10 per prisoner per day to operate, compared to $3 per day at Atlanta.

Gardens planted by families of the original Army post and later by families of the prison guards, fell into neglect after the prison was closed in 1963.

The untended gardens became overgrown and developed into nesting habitat and sanctuary for numerous birds.

In clearing out the overgrowth of the old gardens, workers found that many of the original plants were growing where they had been planted, more than 100 years before.

The workers found heirloom rose hybrids, including a Welsh rose that was believed to be extinct. Many species of roses, succulents, and geraniums are growing among apple and fig trees.

Chapter 7

Shanghaiing Sailors

Clipper ships required a great deal of labor.

San Francisco wasn't the only port where men were "shanghaied" or kidnapped to work as sailors. It mattered not that the individual had little or no sea experience.

The people engaged in this form of kidnapping were known as *crimps*. These crimps flourished in port cities like San Francisco, Portland and Astoria, Oregon.

In the mid nineteenth century there was a severe shortage of experienced sailors on the American west coast.

Once a sailor signed onto a vessel for a voyage, it was illegal for him to leave the ship before the voyage's end. The penalty for doing so was imprisonment under provisions of federal legislation enacted in 1790.

This act was weakened by the Maguire Act of 1895 and the White Act of 1897. It was finally eradicated altogether by the Seaman's Act of 1915.

The practice of shanghaiing began in California because of crews abandoning their ships to head for the gold rush. The shanghaiing practice was made possible through the use of boarding masters.

Boarding masters were paid "by the body". This was a strong incentive to secure a seaman by any means possible.

This set up the stage for the crimp, a boarding master who used trickery, intimidation or violence to put a sailor aboard a ship. The most straightforward method for a crimp to shanghai a man to become a sailor was to render him unconscious.

The crimp would then forge the man's name on the ship's articles and pick up the "blood" money.

In some situations, the boarding master would receive the first two, three or four months of wages of a man he shipped out. Some crimps made as much as $9,500 per year in 1890 dollars. This was equivalent to $260,000 in 2012.

Author Georgia Smith wrote about the shanghaiing of two men in a San Francisco bar one afternoon in the 1890s. Hiram Bailey and his friend Ben (neither one of whom was a sailor) were in a dive on the waterfront.

"Over our drinks, I conveyed to Ben—for Ben knew nothing of sea life—and I but a bit more—that it was common talk about the harbor that the

70

Benares had put to sea with two clergymen, three bartenders, four agricultural laborers—all shanghaied.

But what is the meaning of shanghaied? Inquired my companion.

As I was about the explain, Ben turned and ordered from Calico Jim a small bottle of whiskey.

A little of it does your nerves good, he told me.

I examined the sealing of the cork and found it was a new "untouched" bottle. "No dope in this". I was eighteen.

Calico Jim joined us at the table. He brought his own glass and very suavely invited himself to join our conversation.

I can still remember a strange but pleasant feeling stealing over me whilst taking that swig and there is still silhouetted upon my mind that scoundrel's evil face intently watching me. It never occurred to me why.

Bailey said that he and Ben woke up the next day to a kick in the stomach and orders to heave hard. They were forced to labor at sea for months.

In San Francisco, Joseph "Frenchy" Franklin and George Lewis were long-time crimps. They were elected to the California legislature, an ideal spot to assure that no legislation would be passed that would have a negative impact on their business.

71

The most infamous crimp examples were Jim "Shanghai" Kelly and Johnny "Shanghai Chicken" Devine, both of San Francisco.

Shanghai Kelly kept a boarding house on Pacific or Broadway, depending on the source. He later ran the Boston Boarding House at Broadway and Polk Streets.

His saloon was highly mytholized. Some say the saloon had three trapdoors through which unconscious sailors, whether drugged or knocked in the head, were dumped to spirit away to waiting ships.

Some reports say that Chinatown cigar makers made up special brands of opiates for Shanghai Kelly to give unsuspecting sailors.

There are some stories that claim Jim "Shanghai" Kelly even shipped out corpses and once, a cigar store Indian.

Another story circulating San Francisco was that another crimp, Nikko the Lapp, was a runner for shanghaiier Miss Piggott. Nikko specialized in sewing rats into a dead man's clothing, then dumping the corpse in a bag and delivering it to a ship as a dead-drunk sailor.

The rats made the body twitch in a lifelike manner. The ship captain would realize the body was dead until out to sea.

Shanghai Kelly, himself, was shanghaied by his fellow crimp, Johnny 'Shanghai Chicken" Devine.

The most elaborate Shanghai Kelly story is when three ships lay anchored in the Bay waiting for crews. Kelly decided he would make a lot of money getting crews for all three.

Kelly chartered a paddle-wheeler to throw a birthday bash for himself. He issued a blanket invitation along the waterfront. Ninety people packed into the paddle-wheeler.

As the merry-makers drained the barrels of booze, getting more and more intoxicated, Kelly hoisted drunken party-goers over the side onto each of the three waiting ships.

In 1897, the U.S. Supreme Court decision in Robertson v. Baldwin excluded civilian sailors on merchant ships from the 13th Amendment's protection against involuntary servitude.

Of all the links in the system, the sailor hated the crimp the most. He was the middleman dealing directly with a boardinghouse and contacting ship captains to obtain crews for them. The crimp was a sort of employment agent.

The crimp charged each sailor five dollars for his fee. In addition, the crimp made money by bringing men to a boarding house and again he would get "blood money" from the ship's captain.

No matter how much they hated the system, most sailors could not escape from the system. Only when seamen were scarce could a man get a job on his own initiative.

Shanghaiing flourished openly in San Francisco for sixty years. Politicians who were paid off winked at the issue as repeated reform efforts failed.

"There was too much money to be made," author Richard Dillon said in his book, "Shanghaiing Days".

The crimps worked hand in hand with the "thuggish" boardinghouse masters. Most of the boardinghouses were located on the northern waterfront, along Front and Davis streets from Pacific Avenue north to Filbert Street.

The crimps included both men and women, including the ferocious Miss Piggott who operated a saloon and boardinghouse on Davis Street.

Miss Piggott worked with a crimp named Nikko the Lapp. He would lure an unsuspecting person along her bar until he was standing on top of a trapdoor.

Miss Piggott then poured a cocktail containing equal parts of whisky, brandy and gin, with a nice lacing of laudanum or opium. While the victim was shivering under the impact of the beverage, Miss Piggott leaned across the bar and tapped the victim in the head with a bung-starter. Nikko followed with a blow from a slung shot.

As the prospect crumbled to the floor, Miss Piggott operated a lever behind the bar,, dumping the victim into the basement, where he fell upon a mattress which Miss Piggott thoughtfully provided.

When the victim awoke, he was aboard a ship bound for some foreign port, unknowing as to where he was or how he got there.

Chapter 8

The Fantastic Cable Cars

Andrew Smith Hallidie, inventor of the cable car.

Andrew Smith Hallidie watched in horror as a team of five horses struggled to tug an over-loaded streetcar up Clay Street. When the tired horses could pull the car no higher, on the wet cobblestones, it plunged to the bottom of the hill, dragging the five horses with it to their death.

After witnessing the gruesome accident, Hallidie was convinced the strong cables that he manufactured could be used to replace the horse-drawn streetcars.

Hallidie owned a cable manufacturing plant on the corner of Mason and Chestnut streets. His "wire rope" was used in the designing and building of a suspension bridge across the American River. It was also a mainstay in California's gold mines to pull heavy ore cars out of the underground mines.

The Scotsman made no secret of his desire to eliminate the use of horses. He would place his strong cables underground and power them with steam. Cars would be attached to the cables much like ore buckets in the mines of the Sierra Nevada gold fields.

Hallidie found an unusual alliance to support his idea to build a horseless cable car that would carry passengers up and down the steep San Francisco hillsides.

The support came from the Society for the Prevention of Cruelty to Animals, who claimed that pulling the horse-drawn trams significantly shortened the life of the animals.

Hallidie was born Andrew Smith. He adopted the name Hallidie in honor of his uncle, Sir Andrew Hallidie, who served as a Royal physician to William IV.

Hallidie's father, Andrew Smith, was an engineer and held a patent for the making of wire rope. In 1852, the father and son set sail for California where the father had an interest in some Mariposa County gold mines.

The mining claims proved disappointing and the father returned to England. Young Andrew remained in California. He began working as a gold miner and as a blacksmith, surveyor and builder of bridges.

While working on building a flume at a mine at American Bar, Hallidie groused over the rapid rate of wear on the ropes used to lower cars of rock from the mine to the mill.

The ropes were wearing out in 75 days. Hallidie improvised machinery to make a replacement wire rope that would last for two years. The process was successful and he began the manufacture of wire rope in California.

Hallidie abandoned mining and returned to San Francisco. He commenced making wire rope in a building at Mason and Chestnut streets using the machinery he made at American Bar.

During 1861-62, Hallidie contracted to build a bridge across the Bear, Trinity, Stanislaus and Tuolumne rivers. A year later, he built a bridge across the Fraser River, 10 miles upstream of Yale at Alexandra in British Columbia.

Also in 1863, he married Martha Elizabeth Woods. He became a U.S. citizen in 1864. Hallidie then gave up bridge building to promote his wire rope manufacturing.

He invented the Hallidie ropeway, a form of aerial tramway used to transport ore and other materials across mountainous areas. He installed a number of installations and received a patent for the process.

Hallidie also gained the support of three friends, Henry Davis, James Moffat, and Joseph Britton, who could envision Hallidie's description of his cable railway.

The four men, in 1872, formed a corporation and obtained a franchise to build a street railway in Clay Street. Although they offered stock in the corporation to the public, money was slow in materializing.

Eventually, Hallidie himself put up $20,000 for the venture. His partners added another $40,000. The Clay Street Bank, in which the corporation maintained its office, advanced another $30,000.

The contract with the city stated the line must be operational by August 1, 1873. Hallidie tested the first cable car at 4 a.m. on August 2, 1873. It was on Clay Street in San Francisco.

Even though he was a day late, the cable car trials received great approval. The new company began public service on September 1, 1873.

His idea for a steam engine powered, cable driven, rail system was conceived in 1869. Clay Street Hill Railroad was the sole cable car company on the streets of San Francisco for four years.

In 1877, California Street Cable Railroad developed its own version. This was followed by California Street Cable Railroad in 1878, Geary Street, Park & Ocean Railroad in 1880, Presidio and Ferries Railroad in 1882, Market Street Cable Railway in 1883, Ferries & cliff House Railway in 1888 and Omnibus Railroad & Cable Company in 1889.

All told, the cable companies laid down 53 miles of tract, stretching from the Ferry Building to the Presidio, to Golden Gate Park, to the Castro, to Mission.

Each strand of Hallidie's high quality cable had a thickness of .062 inches and the completed cable had a tensile strength of 160,000 pounds.

A San Francisco Cable Car

The working parts of the power system required grips, brakes, trucks for the trams, and other safety features

The greatest obstacle facing the quartet was designing the patterns for the working parts of the power system, the grips, brake, and truck for the trams. The design had dealt also with the suspension, carriage and propulsion of the cable.

The deadline date drew ever closer for the cable car builders. The slot to hold the cable was completed only two days before the experimental run was scheduled.

Eventually, Hallidie himself put up $20,000 for the venture. His partners added another $40,000. The Clay Street Bank, in which the corporation maintained its office, advanced another $30,000.

A powerhouse had been built at the corner of Clay and Leavenworth streets, a full city block beyond the point designated as the terminus for the line. The cable drums were activated by steam engines fired by great Scotch boilers. After 1906, electricity was used to power the cable drums.

The first run for San Francisco's first cable car was set for five o'clock in the morning on the same day the franchise expired. It was a foggy morning, and many of the spectators feared the cable car's brakes would not hold on the rails that were wet from the drizzling fog.

Fog shrouded the area and muffled the sounds spectators expected to hear. Then, as if magically, the mists rolled away. At the farthest terminus of the line a cable car appeared, upright and intact.

Hallidie's experimental run was completed. His next worry was to conduct a run in which paying passengers rode the new mechanical marvel. Word spread around the city that the cable car was an overwhelming success.

Another run this time with passengers was set for the afternoon and would include city dignitaries. Hallidie adapted a passenger car with lateral banquettes or benches to be towed behind the power-governed dummy.

The seating capacity of the dummy and the trailer was only 25 persons. But when the cable car started on that initial run everyone wanted to share the ride. Ninety persons jammed aboard. Over-crowding of cable cars still exists today, as city folks and tourists alike clamber aboard already full cars.

The popularity of the cable cars sent the company's stock spiraling, even though the fare was only five cents. The original sixty thousand-dollar investment earned three thousand dollars every thirty days, better than sixty percent per annum.

Chapter 9

Jack London

Jack London

John Griffith Chaney, better known as Jack London, was born in San Francisco on January 12, 1876,
He began calling himself Jack as a boy. He was the son of Flora Wellman, an unwed mother. His mother married John London, a Civil War veteran while Jack was a boy.

London grew up as a working class citizen. He carved out a hardscrabble life as a teen. He rode freight trains, pirated oysters, shoveled coal, worked on a sailing ship, and in a cannery.

His free time was consumed by books. He would hunker down at libraries soaking up novels and travel books.

Jack London in his adult years.

His mother saw the announcement of a writing contest in a local paper. She pushed Jack to submit his sailing-ship voyage.

Armed with an eighth-grade education, London won the $25 first prize, winning out over college students from Berkeley and Stanford. It was an eye-opening experience for London. He decided to dedicate his life to writing short stories.

Getting published initiated a great discipline in London. From that time forward, he made it a practice to write at least a thousand words every day.

By the age of 27, he had gained an amount of fame and fortune. His *Call of the Wild* told the story of a Yukon sled dog. London was a prolific writer and published 50 books over the last 16 years of his life.

In his novel, *John Barleycorn*, he detailed his battle with alcohol.

In 1893, he weathered a harrowing trip aboard a sailing vessel. A typhoon nearly took out the 17-year-old London and his crew.

As a child, his mother, Flora, suffered from typhoid fever. The disease left her nearly blind and hairless. She suffered repeated bouts of depression.

When she was 25 years old, she moved to San Francisco, which at the time was over-flowing with gold miners and railroad magnates. She gave piano lessons to support herself.

In 1874, she moved in with William Chaney, an astrologer who encouraged her fascination with spiritualism. Together they ran an astrology parlor. Flora would receive money to communicate with the dead and send messages to the loved ones of the deceased.

She gave birth to Jack, but was never sure that Chaney was his father. She referred to him as her "badge of shame".

His birth almost killed her and she was never able to care for him. She sent him to a wet nurse, an ex-slave named Virginia Prentiss. She took the place of Jack's mother for the first eight months of his life.

A few months later, Flora met and married John London. Flora's restlessness, mood swings, hysterical breakdowns, and feigned heart attacks blighted the life of the entire family. It was especially hard on young Jack.

As Jack grew older, he became tough from fighting off bullies. Despite his small size, he garnered a reputation for his cunning ability to brawl.

At 14, he graduated from grammar school. Because his family couldn't afford to send him to high school, he worked in a canning factory.

Even at this young age, books opened up a whole new world for him. However, the more he canned pickles, the more he craved escape. He turned to alcohol to get away from the real world.

When he got drunk in local saloons, he met men of the sea—sailors, sealers, whalers, and harpooners. When an opportunity arose to become an oyster-pirate, he grabbed it. He roamed the San Francisco Bay, stealing oysters from other people's oyster farms.

Ironically, his next job was working for the local fish patrol chasing poachers.

Jack spent a year tramping around the U.S. before finding himself once again in his mother's kitchen. He resolved to give up his vagrant ways and go back to high school.

Jack developed interests in political theory, especially Socialism. His involvement in the Socialist Labor Party got him kicked out of school.

He continued studying, preparing for the entrance exams to the University of California at Berkeley.

He was accepted by the university, but dropped out after six months. He was disappointed by the experience. At this point he began pursuing writing in earnest, working at a laundry to support himself.

He maintained his interest in social issues. He ran several times as a candidate for the Mayor of Oakland on the Socialist ticket. He was roundly defeated each time.

Jack was instrumental in breaking the taboo over leprosy and popularizing Hawaii as a tourist spot. He was a popular figure, but he always used this pulpit to endorse socialism, women's suffrage and eventually, prohibition.

He finally got his big break with *Odyssey of the North*, a short story. The story received critical acclaim for its virility and vivid descriptions. That same year, Jack married Bessie Maddem.

Unfortunately, Jack believed fervently in natural selection. His marriage was based on that premise rather than romantic love.

While his career soared, his marriage didn't He and Bessie had a daughter, Joan. But London began spending more and more time with friends than he did with his wife. He openly had affairs and traveled a great deal. A second daughter was born in 1902.

In 1903, he wrote *The Call of the Wild*. It was published and Jack separated from his wife Bessie.

In 1904, he covered the Russo-Japanese War for Hearst Newspapers. He also published *The Sea Wolf*. It turned into one of his most successful books.

He married his former secretary Charmian Kittredge in 1905. A year later he began building a sailing vessel which he named *Snark*. He and Charmian sailed around the world and London wrote extensively about their time on the trip (*The Cruise of the Snark*).

While he was one of the highest paid writers of his time, he was terrible at managing money. He was always short of cash.

London died of kidney failure on November 21, 1916.

Chapter 10

The Hippies

A Hippie Bus

The Hippie culture was pretty much centered on the belief, "If it feels good, do it." And most of them did just that.

There had been two world wars and a depression, all within a 30-year period.

It was the hippies who took the counter-culture movement out of the coffee shops and onto the campuses around the country. Berkeley became the center of the movement.

The word Hippie derives from the term "Hipster" and was initially used to describe beatniks who had moved into the Haight-Ashbury district of San Francisco.

A gathering of San Francisco's Flower Children

Sit-ins and protests were staged. The beat generation was angry at the injustices in the country. They didn't like the racism, the poverty and the lack of women's rights.

The movement started small and then grew—and grew—and grew.

The escalation of the Vietnam War played heavily in the Hippie movement. More and more young people were going to Vietnam. It was a war that was considered unjust.

Peace became a common goal of the movement and the ranks of Hippies swelled to huge proportions.

The music of the Hippie period pretty much came out of the folk music of musicians coming out

90

of the Great Depression. Pete Seeger and Woody Guthrie were prime idols.

Joan Baez, Bob Dylan and Arlo Guthrie brought the folk music up to date in the 1960s.

The primary tenet of the Hippie generation was about being happy, not about what others thought you should be.

Hippies were dissatisfied with what their parents had built for them. If they had only looked around they might have realized their parents had built the greatest booming economy the world had ever seen.

Established institutions were abhorred by the Beatniks. They called them "The Establishment", "Big Brother", and "The Man".

The hippie generation believed that the dominant mainstream culture was all corrupt. They wanted to replace it with a Utopian society.

Drugs crept into the Hippie culture. The generation praised free love and sexual liberation, especially for the women.

Marijuana and LSD were integrated into the Hippie culture. Contrary to popular thinking, Hippies tended to avoid the harder drugs such as heroin and amphetamines because they considered them harmful and addictive.

Brightly colored, ragged clothes, tie-dyed t-shirts, beads, sandals (or barefoot) all were used to differentiate the Hippie from the conventional class.

Hippie men grew long hair and cultivated beards and mustaches. Women wore little or no makeup and often went "bra-less" or shirtless.

A Hippie scene in San Fancisco

The entire Hippie generation adopted the peace symbol as their logo. The VW bus became their main mode of transportation. The buses were painted with colorful graphics. Many hitch hiked to get to Hippie events.

At the end of summer 1967, the Hippie movement came to an end. An effigy was burned in Golden Gate Park.

The Haight-Ashbury scene had deteriorated. The district could not accommodate the influx of hundreds of thousands of Hippies. Malnourishment, disease, and drug addiction grew prominent in the Haight community.

Crime and violence escalated out of sight as homeless drug addicted Hippies stole to survive and drug dealers moved in to control the drug trade.

Chapter 11

Herb Caen

Herb Caen

S an Francisco lost a pillar of strength
when its revered pundit Herb Caen died.
Caen was the dessert the people ate first

when they opened the pages of San Francisco Chronicle.

His was a continuous love letter to San Francisco, a town he both respected and adored during his nearly 60 years as the city's most revered columnist.

It was Herb Caen that San Franciscans woke up to each morning. Many read the column either "hoping" or "dreading" the possibility that they might be mentioned in Caen's daily posting.

Caen was born April 3, 1916 in Sacramento. He liked to point out that his parents spent the summer before in San Francisco. He began writing a column in high school called *Corridor Gossip*. He also covered sports events for the Sacramento Union.

In 1936, he wrote a radio column for the San Francisco Chronicle. When that column was discontinued, Caen proposed a daily column on the City of San Francisco itself.

"It's News to Me" first appeared July 5, 1938. A Caen colleague wrote this about the man;

> *On good days his column offers everything you expect from an entire newspaper—in just 25 or so items, 1,000 or so words.*

A good example would have been his column of Feb. 14, 1966. There the reader learned that Willie Mays' home was on the market for $110,000. The Bank of America now owned the block where it wanted to build its headquarters. *"Dr. Zhivago"* director David Lean was in town. Meanwhile,

"Mike Connelly is ready to concede that the situation in Vietnam is complex: 'Even my cab driver can't come up with a solution.'"

Herb Caen is responsible for coining the term *"beatnik"* in 1958. He popularized the term *hippie* during San Francisco's 1967 Summer of Love.

He used playful terms such as *Frisbeetarianism* and ribbed nearby Berkeley as *Berserkeley.*

Caen doted on colorful personalities who regularly made their appearance in his daily musings. Among his favorites was Edsel Ford Fung, who was San Francisco's rudest waiter.

Ford became famous for berating and insulting the customers, all with tongue in cheek.

Caen had an army of reliable tipsters to keep him abreast of the goings on in San Francisco.

Herb Caen was a very quotable writer, as witnessed by the following:

> *A city is where you can sign a petition, boo the chief justice, fish off a pier, gaze at a hippopotamus, buy a flower at the corner, or get a good hamburger or a bad girl at 4 a.m. A city is where sirens make white streaks of sound in the sky and foghorns speak in dark grays. San Francisco is such a city.*

> *A city is a crazy concrete jungle whose people at the end of each day somehow make a small step ahead against terrible odds.*

A city is not gauged by its length and width, but by the broadness of its vision and the height of its dreams.

The only thing wrong with immortality is that it tends to go on forever.

Just two days in Manhattan and you find yourself looking for a place to wash your handkerchief after you wipe your forehead and it comes away black. Is there a dirtier or more fascinating city anywhere in the land? The answer to both parts of the question has to be positively negative.

A man begins cutting his wisdom teeth the first time he bites off more than he can chew.

I have a memory like an elephant. I remember every elephant I've ever met.

Cockroaches and socialites are the only things that stay up all night and eat anything.

A city is a state-of-mind, of taste, of opportunity. A city is a market place where ideas are traded, opinions clash and eternal conflict may produce eternal truths.

Old San Francisco—the one so many nostalgics yearn for—had buildings that related well to each other.

A good column is one that sells paper. It doesn't matter how beautifully it is written and how much you admire the author...if it doesn't sell any papers, it's not a good column. It's a terrible yardstick to use, but in the newspaper business, that's the whole thing.

When a place advertises itself as 'World Famous', you may be sure it isn't.

The trouble with born-again Christians is that they are an even bigger pain the second time around.

I tend to live in the past because most of my life is there.

Logic is no answer to passion.

One thing that Herb Caen did for his readers was that he left his city in better shape each day.

Chapter 12

The Barbary Coast

There was never a shortage of customers for Barbary Coast establishments.

T he Barbary Coast in the late 19th and early 20th centuries wasn't hard to describe. It was simply a *Red Light District.*

It was born during the 1849 Gold Rush and centered around a three-block stretch of Pacific Street, between Montgomery and Stockton Streets.

The massive infusion of *Forty-Niners* just naturally led to a place where the gold miners could get away from the dust and grime of the gold fields.

The population of San Francisco soared from 492 persons in 1847 to more than 25,000 people in 1849.

A natural outlet for the frustrations and disappointments of the gold miners was the raucous and wild debauchery of The Barbary Coast.

There the miners could find a wide assortment of entertainment. There were the typical saloons, dance hall girls, casinos and the always desired *ladies of the evening.* Gold miners could get a hot bath which they couldn't count on in the gold fields.

While principally associated with female prostitution, Barbary Coast dives offered crude burlesque performances, "leg-shows", belly dancing, and coin operated "peep shows" that allowed patrons to watch prostitutes ply their trade.

In his book, *California As I Saw It,* William S. McCollum wrote a dim view of the women prostitutes as a whole.

> *The Senoritas are not fascinating, because they are not pretty—they are very willing to be gazed at, however, and are inclined to coquetry. I must confess I prefer something lighter—and less greasy—more graceful and less indolent, and above all, something which can speak English.*

The irrepressible Mark Twain wrote about the Nicaraguan women who had landed in San Francisco.

> *They are virtuous, according to their lights, but I guess that their lights are a little dim.*

Another author painted this picture of the women from Paraguay.

Everybody smokes in Paraguay, and nearly every female above thirteen years of age chews. Only imagine yourself about to kiss a magnificent little Hebe, arrayed in satin and flashing with diamonds; she puts you back with one delicate hand, while with the fair tapered fingers of the other she draws forth from her mouth a brownish-black roll of tobacco, quite two inches long and looking like a monstrous grub. She deposits the delicate morsel on the rim of your sombrero, puts up her face and is ready for a salute.

A Sacramento woman had this to say about the lust in men.

Every man thought every woman in that day a beauty. Even I have had men come forty miles over the mountains just to look at me, and I never was called a handsome woman in my best day, even by my most ardent admirers.

Though there was scarce evidence of commercialized homosexual activity on the Barbary Coast, there was enough cross dressing going on to alarm the Board of Supervisors.

101

The diligent supervisors added an ordinance to the Health Code in 1903.

Anyone is forbidden to appear on any public highway in clothing not belonging to or usually worn by his or her sex.

There was usually at least one murder every night in the Barbary Coast and scores of robberies. Police refused to walk the streets alone. They walked either in pairs or in groups.

Drug addicts could buy cocaine or morphine at an all night Grant Street drugstore for two or three times the price of a beer.

San Francisco hit its peak alcohol consumption in the 1890s with more than 3,000 licensed bars, and another 2,000 unlicensed bars.

Despite their efforts during the early twentieth century, San Francisco moralists made very little progress in a city where the odds were so great. It was a city where sexual permissiveness and outright political corruption prevailed.

Neither the San Francisco Police Department nor any mayoral administration during this period seriously enforced the state and local ordinances outlawing prostitution or "lewd, indecent, or obscene acts."

When the police department did crack down on prostitution, it merely discouraged prostitutes from plying their trade on specific streets or in certain neighborhoods. The police was simply relocating the industry while tacitly approving of it.

In a saloon called the *Fierce Grizzly*, a preacher showed up one day hoping to get some material for future sermons.

The bartender served a milk cocktail, mixed with gin or whisky.

"What is that?" the preacher asked.

"Just milk," the bartender said.

The preacher tasted the concoction.

"Ah" he exclaimed, "What a glorious cow."

It was not until the 1860s that sailors gave the district the name, The Barbary Coast, a term borrowed from the Barbary Coast of North Africa where pirates and slave traders plied their trades.

The San Francisco Barbary Coast provided a haven for all kinds. There were petty thieves, the house burglar, the tramp, the whoremonger, lewd women, cutthroats, and murderers all found here.

Protection from the enforcement of the laws lined the pockets of more than a few police officers and at least one mayor in 1906.

In 1901, Eugene Schmitz, president of the Musician's Union, won election as mayor of San Francisco.

Attorney Abe Reuf injected himself into San Francisco politics and wrote the Union Labor Party's platform.

It was well-known that Abe Reuf was the "unpaid attorney" for the mayor's office and the real power behind the throne. Reuf's law practice prospered as new clients hired him even when they had no use for his legal services.

Abe Reuf

One of Reuf's first arrangements was with the Pacific Telephone and Telegraph Company. Theodore V. Halsey, AT&T's confidential political agent, began delivering $250 a month in cash to Reuf.

The money was not for Reuf to conduct court cases, but ostensibly for advice on matters if municipal law. Such understandings became the norm for Reuf.

Abraham Reuf became a name synonymous with municipal corruption. Reuf divided the money he received in half. He pocketed half of it and passed the rest on to the Mayor and his ally on the Board of Supervisors, James L. Gallagher.

Gallagher divided the money he received among the 16 supervisors who were on the take. When a specific decision needed to be taken, Reuf would inform his colleagues in a private caucus meeting prior to the open supervisors meeting.

A year after the 1906 earthquake hit San Francisco, corruption and graft prosecutions began. Reuf was sent to San Quentin for a five year sentence for his corruption charges.

In 1911, there was a shift in San Francisco's dominating political party. A new mayor, James "Sunny Jim" Rolph was elected to his first of 10 terms.

He came in with a new board of supervisors and was committed to reforming the Barbary Coast District. The San Francisco Examiner echoed the need for such a crusade, saying on its editorial pages that The Barbary Coast should be "wiped out".

Ten days later, the Police Commission adopted rules forbidding dancing in any establishment which served alcohol. Some drinking establishments fired their female employees and became straight saloons.

Some saloons closed while others moved their businesses to other districts. In 1917, the brothels were closed down due to the Red Light Abatement Act.

By that time, the excitement of the Barbary Coast was gone.

Chapter 13

The Coit Tower

The Lillie Coit Tower

At the age of eight, Lillie Hitchcock was trapped when fire raged through a building she and two other youngsters were exploring.

Lillie stood in the midst of a ring of flames. She watched as John Boynton, a substitute fire fighter on San Francisco's Knickerbocker Number Five fire company, hacked a hole through the roof.

Boynton lowered himself on a rope, and carried Lillie on his back while clambering hand-over-hand back up the rope to safety. The other youngsters perished in the fire.

Lillie Coit

From then on, Lillie's affection for Knickerbocker No. 5 continued to grow.

At age fifteen, the fire company had a short staff on the ropes as it raced to a fire on Telegraph Hill. Because of the shortage of manpower, the engine was falling behind.

It would be humiliating to the firemen if Manhattan No. 2 or Howard No. 3 beat Knickerbocker to the fire. It was then that Lillie, on her way home from school, took action.

Lillie tossed her books to the sidewalk and dashed to a vacant place on the rope. At the same time, Lillie cried out to the bystanders, "Come on, you men! Everybody pull and we'll beat 'em!"

And the bystanders did come and pull and Knickerbocker No. 5 hurled up the slope and put "first water" on the fire.

A view of San Francisco as seen from the Coit Tower.

From that day on, Lillie caught the spirit of the Volunteer Firemen, and they in turn responded. There was never a gala parade in which Lillie was not seen atop Knickerbocker No. 5. She was, literally, the patroness of all the firemen of her city.

Lillie was always something of a "tomboy". As a child, she romped in short frocks and was fascinated by the red shirt and warlike helmets worn by firemen. She gloried in the excitement of a big blaze.

While still in her teens, Lillie rushed to the scene of every fire when she heard the fire bell toll its alarms. She came to be regarded as a mascot by the firemen.

On October 3, 1863, Lillie was elected an honorary member of the Knickerbocker Company, and always regarded that honor as the proudest of her life. She wore the numeral and the gold badge the firemen presented her with all her costumes.

Lillie would leave whatever she was doing to attend a fire. Once she left a wedding party in which she was a bridesmaid.

The Hitchcock's were considered valued members of San Francisco Society, and her parents, especially her mother, agonized over the actions of Lillie.

When Lillie's father, Dr. Charles Hitchcock heard about Lillie driving a team of horses at their Calistoga summer home, he didn't try to stop her. Instead, he hired Colonel Clark Foss, a noted stagecoach driver, to give her lessons.

According to one account, Lillie would often drive groups of her suitors, usually at breakneck speed, to the White Sulphur Springs Hotel. Then, often as not, she beat the young men at poker while smoking cigars and helping to polish off a bottle of bourbon.

Howard Coit first saw Lillie when she was riding Knickerbocker No. 5 back from a fire. "I was surprised," he said later, "that she was incandescent rather than beautiful."

When Lillie sighted Coit, it was said to be love at first sight. They eloped in 1869, angering Lillie's mother who felt the young stockbroker was not good enough for her daughter.

Coit died in 1885, but he and Lillie had already been separated for five years. Their marriage had been fraught with suspicion and jealousy.

In 1904, Lillie reported that an assassin bent on killing her broke into her room while she was

110

entertaining a Major McClurg. The major boldly defended her and subdued the assassin, but McClurg later died. The assassin, ruled insane by the courts, was assigned to a padded cell.

Lillie was so shaken by the event that she moved to Paris, where she lived for 20 years. It was not until the assassin died that Lillie returned to her beloved San Francisco.

Lillie Coit died in San Francisco July 22, 1929, at the age of 86. She left one-third of her fortune to the city "to be expended in an appropriate manner for the purpose of adding to the beauty of the city which I have always loved."

The executors of her will, several years after her death, decided to erect a memorial tower in her honor and also as a memorial tribute to San Francisco's firemen.

This novel 180-foot cylindrical tower stands atop Telegraph Hill. Many say the tower is shaped like the nozzle of a fire hose. Historians say the similarity is coincidental.

A family mausoleum holds the remains of Lillie (she was cremated). Beside the niche where her ashes are stored is a khaki fire jacket, a coiled fire hose, and a brass fire hose nozzle.

Coit Tower stands 210 feet tall. It was built in 1933 using Lillie Hitchock's bequest ot beautify the city of San Francisco. She left one-third of her estate to the city for civic beautification.

The San Francisco Board of Supervisors proposed that Coit's bequest be used to build a road at Lake Merced. This proposal was shot down by the Coit estate executors. They said the board should find a way to use the money on a memorial that would be an entity and not a unit of public development.

Chapter 14

Sally Stanford

Sally Stanford in front of her bar at Valhalla.

No California madam was quite as famous as Sally Stanford who maintained perhaps the classiest whorehouse in San Francisco during the 1930s. Her house became so famous a landmark that it was included on the city's sightseeing tours.

Sally Stanford was born Mabel Janice Busby in Oregon in 1903. She came to San Francisco in 1924. She changed her name while walking down

Kearney Street one day and saw a newspaper headline, "Stanford Wins Big Game".

"That's for me!" she told herself. "I'm going after big game."

A story is told about a young policeman, bursting into her establishment and announcing, "I'm bustin' this place!"

"Before you do that buster," Sally coolly told him, "I suggest you go out to the kitchen and talk to your dad—we were just having a cup of coffee."

Sally operated an elegant bordello at 1144 Pine Street from 1940 to 1949 in a house designed by architect Stanford White.

In her autobiography, Sally wrote, "Madaming is the sort of thing that just happens to you—like getting a battlefield commission or becoming dean of women at Stanford University."

In 1967, Sally made a surprise appearance at the men's luncheon during the California Jaycees Annual convention. She paraded into the San Francisco Hilton ballroom wearing a feathered boa flowing down over an ornate, floor-length gown.

Seated at the head table were Senator Edward Kennedy, Mayor Joseph Alioto, Attorney Melvin Belli and the newly elected California Jaycees president, Drew Frohlich.

Greeting each of them with a hug and a buss on the cheek, Sally then took the podium. She brought the house down by naming each and every one of them as a past or present customer.

Sally's formal education ended with the third grade. Still, she was a sharp and intelligent businesswoman.

Sally convinced golfers at the local golf course to let her work as their caddy. She was only seven years old at the time. Her mother was a teacher and her father was an incompetent farmer who died while Sally was still small.

At a young age, Sally fell in with some bad companions. Her first run-in with the law involved a sentencing to the Oregon State Prison while she was 16 years old. Her crime was helping a male cohort cash checks he'd stolen from a Medford, Oregon lumber mill.ooooooooooooooooooooooooooooooooooooooooooooo oooooooooooooooo999999999999

Stanford learned the bootlegging trade from her cellmates. It served her well. After her release from prison, she opened a speakeasy in Ventura, California where she served salted roast chicken and bootlegged booze.

It was her beginning at building her personal wealth. Her speakeasy was one of the most popular places in town.

She was 21-years old when she arrived in San Francisco. She started her career as a madam by investing her money in a hotel at 695 O'Farrell Street in the Tenderloin section of the city.

Sally then added a house at 610 Leavenworth Street, also in the Tenderloin. She created an elegant interior and atmosphere by filling it with beautiful and professional prostitutes.

One of her most famous bordellos was at 1144 Pine Street on Nob Hill, considered the swankiest neighborhood in San Francisco at the time.

In it was a Roman bathtub measuring nine feet in diameter. The house was demolished in 1961 to build condominiums.

Sally Stanford's house at 1144 Pine St., San Francisco.

Wealthy and influential men from all over the world made up Stanford's clientele. There were shahs, princes, movie stars, national dignitaries and California state and local government officials.

Columnist Herb Caen, in writing about the United Nations, said, "The United Nations was founded at Sally Stanford's whorehouse."

It is said that many of the actual negotiations and decisions were made in the parlor of her 1144 Pine Street House.

In her autobiography, *The Lady of the House*, Sally wrote about a famous movie star who ordered two girls be sent to his room at the Fairmont Hotel at the top of Nob Hill.

The girls returned to Stanford's brothel and reported the rough treatment they'd received from the actor. When he later requested Sally's girls, she flatly refused.

She said that Errol Flynn, Frank Sinatra and Humphrey Bogart were customers. While she always welcomed Flynn and Sinatra, she said that Bogart was a foul mouthed, pugnacious drunk who came around to belittle and insult the girls.

Sally used several aliases during her years as a madam. At various times she was known as Marcia Busby, Marcia Owen or Marcia Wells. While she made her legal name Sally Stanford in 1971, she kept her phone listings in the name of Marcia Owen for her San Francisco residences and for her 50-acre ranch in Sonoma County.

Stanford had some gentlemen friends of her own, a few of whom she married. Her first husband was Daniel Goodan, he second was her attorney, Ernest Spagnoli, and her third was to Louis Rapp, which lasted 12 years.

Her fourth marriage was to Robert Gump, the grandson of Solomon Gump, founder of the famous San Francisco import emporium on Post Street.

This marriage was highly publicized. Gump claimed it had taken him two years to convince her to marry him. The marriage lasted nine months.

Her fifth and last marriage was in 1954 to Robert Kenna, operator of a Fresno trucking company. He later was manager of Sally's Valhalla restaurant in Sausalito. This marriage lasted two years.

Sally later said, "One's better off just being a friend. Then you do things because you want to. When you're married it's a duty."

New York's famous madam, Polly Adler, once visited Sally. Adler told Sally, "You know the madam's lament—everybody goes upstairs but us."

After police closed her down in 1949, Sally opened the Valhalla restaurant in Sausalito. She later was elected to the City Council and even served as mayor of the town.

Sally died in Marin County Hospital on February 1, 1982. She was 78-years old.

Chapter 15

The U.S. Mint

The U.S. Mint in San Francisco

When gold started pouring in from the gold fields in 1849, it overwhelmed the U.S. Mint in Philadelphia. The mint could not turn all of the gold into coins fast enough to keep up with the flow.

U.S. President Millard Fillmore recommended that a branch of the United States Mint be built in California. Congress approved the plan in 1852. The mint opened its doors in 1854 and began converting miners' gold into coins..

By December of the first year, it produced $4,084,207 in gold pieces. It outgrew its small brick building and in 1874, it moved to an imposing new structure with walls of stone. It resembled a Greek temple.

The mint's production of coins was uninterrupted for 32 years.

This U.S. Mint Building was opened in 1874.

The solid construction of the new U.S. mint building, with its walls of stone, allowed it to withstand the pressures of the 1906 earthquake. The building is known affectionately as "The Granite Lady".

This nickname may be something of a misnomer in that most of the building is made from sandstone. While the base/basement is made of granite, the entire external and upper stories are made of sandstone. The Granite Lady sobriquet still stuck.

The building sat on a concrete and granite foundation, designed to thwart tunneling into its vaults. At the time of the fire following the 1906 earthquake, the vaults held $300 million, a third of the United States gold reserves.

The Mint was the only financial institution capable of operating immediately after the 1906 earthquake disaster. It became the treasury for disaster relief funds.

The old mint was open to visitors until 1993. In 2003, the federal government sold the structure to the city of San Francisco for one dollar—an 1879 silver dollar that was struck at the mint—for use as a historical museum.

In 1968, the San Francisco Mint took over most proof coinage production from the Philadelphia Mint. Since 1875, the San Francisco Mint has been used only for proof coinage—the exception being from 1979-1981 when it produced the Susan B. Anthony dollar. It also minted a portion of the pennies made in the early 1980s.

The dollars bear a mintmark of an "S", but the cents are indistinguishable from those minted at Philadelphia.

The U.S. Minute provides the following statistics on its output:

●Total number of small cents ever minted in San Francisco: $6,027,667,039 (face value $60,276.670)

●Total number of nickels ever minted in San Francisco: 1,076,486,848 (face value $53,824,342)

●Total number of dimes ever minted in San Francisco: 952,971, 374 (face value $95,297,137)

●Total number of quarters ever minted in San Francisco: 670,669,691 (face value $167,667,423)

●Total number of dollars ever minted in San Francisco: 499,024,906 (face value $499,024,906)

Chapter 16

Fisherman's Wharf

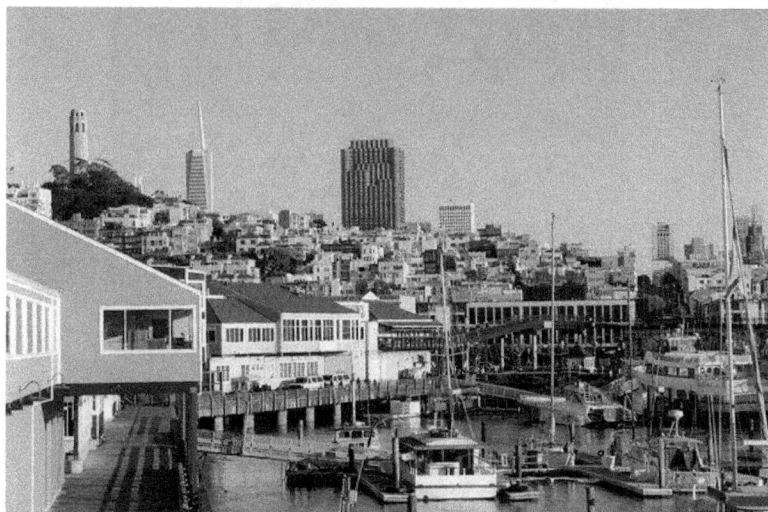

Fisherman's Wharf

Once known as *Little Italy*, Fisherman's Wharf is the busiest tourist spot in the city. It has a wax museum and Ghirardelli Square and is home to more than 130 stores and unique restaurants.

Italian Achille Paladini came to San Francisco during the gold rush. He sold Dungeness crab and other seafood to the gold miners that rushed to San Francisco to make their fortune hunting gold.

This sign greets the visitors to Fisherman's Wharf in San Francisco.

Dungeness crab is the highlight of Fisherman's Wharf.

Sea lions at Pier 39 on Fisherman's Wharf

Paladini made a fortune at his trade. Most of the gold seekers ended their treasure hunting by being broke.

The big highlight at Fisherman's Wharf is the Dungeness crab. While this delicacy is found all along the West Coast from Alaska to Mexico, San Francisco Bay became a major hub for its sales. San Francisco was the only seaport where Dungeness crab was marketed regularly in mass quantities.

In the late 1800s, three to four medium-size crabs sold for a total of twenty five cents.

After two centuries of fishing in the Bay, Dungeness crab is now scarce. The catastrophic 1971 Pacific oil spill contaminated the Bay's waters.

A colony of sea lions moved onto Pier 39, where they lie, soaking up the sun on the wooden docks where boats used to dock. The frolicking sea lions are true crowd pleasers. Some shops sell bait for visitors to feed to the sea lions.

The California sea lions are known for both their playfulness and their annoying barking. Male sea lions will reach 850 pounds and measure up to seven feet in length.

The females grow to about 220 pounds and grow to some six feet in length.

Chapter 17

Treasure Island

Treasure Island

Treassure Island belies its name. It is a man-made island built with landfill. It was built in 1936-37 for the 1939 Golden Gate International Exposition World's Fair.

The San Francisco neighborhood that includes Treasure Island extends far into San Francisco Bay and includes a tip of Alameda Island.

Prior to the island's construction by the Federal Government, *Yerba Buena Shoals* consisted of rock. It had less than 27 feet clearance and was a shipping hazard.

The U.S. Army Corps of Engineers constructed the 404-acre Treasure Island to provide a short-term site for the Golden Gate International Exposition (World's Fair).

Treasure Island is an entirely man-made island constructed of rock and mud fill placed over shallow areas at the northern shore of Yerba Buena Island.

After it was completed, it was connected to Yerba Buena Island by a narrow causeway at the island's southwest corner.

Most buildings were built as temporary structures, with the intent to convert the site into a permanent airport for San Francisco when the exposition closed.

The island was built by dumping 260,000 tons of rock in the shoals to form an island-causeway perimeter. Approximately 23 feet of dredged bay sand filled the interior of the island. The sand was mitigated from salt and then 50,000 cubic yards of topsoil was used to plant 4,000 trees, 70,000 shrubs, and 700,000 flowering plants.

The Magic Isle of the World's Fair opened February 18, 1939. Inside the walled city were several courts: A central Court of Honor, a Court of the East, a Port of Trade Winds and a Court of Pacifica.

There was also a 12,000 car parking lot and a 40-acre lot of carnival rides and side shows. When the World's Fair was over, Treasure Island was taken over by the U.S. Navy.

In 1941 the United States Navy began using Treasure Island as a Navy reception center.

Following World War II, the Navy transformed Treasure Island into a training facility. To do so, the Navy demolished dozens of the temporary structures to allow new construction.

The Navy band stationed at Treasure Island was one of more than 100 Navy bands of African American musicians. The band was popular throughout the San Francisco area.

Band members were recruited to serve "for the duration" at Treasure Island at a starting pay of $66 per month.

The band played for morning colors, at bond rallies and ship launchings. A smaller band, a "Swing Ensemble" taken from the larger band, was known as the "Shipmates of Rhythm" and was considered one of the best bands in the Navy.

The Navy closed Naval Station Treasure Island in 1997. The Treasure Island Development Authority took over as caretaker for the island.

The Treasure Island Development Authority is proposing redevelopment of portions of the naval station that is still owned by the Navy.

The proposal includes the development of 8,000 residential units and up to 140,000 acres of commercial and retail space.

Chapter 18

San Francisco's Sourdough Bread

Master Baker Fernando Padilla apprenticed under Boudin Bakery owner "Papa Steve" Giraudo at 17.

As much as San Franciscans would like to claim it, sourdough bread did not originate in San Francisco. The city can certainly claim leading place for keeping sourdough bread popular.

The person who hasn't heard of San Francisco sourdough has led a sheltered life indeed.

San Francisco Sourdough

Sourdough is believed to have originated in ancient Egypt around 1500 BC. It may have been the first form of leavening available for bakers.

Baker's yeast is not useful as a leavening agent for rye bread, which is the popular grain in the northern part of Europe. Rye does not contain enough gluten.

French bakers brought sourdough techniques to Northern California during the California Gold Rush.

San Francisco sourdough is the most famous sourdough bread made in the United States. San Francisco has remained in continuous production of sourdough bread since 1849.

Some bakeries, such as Boudin Bakery, trace their sourdough starters back to California's Gold Rush period. San Francisco sourdough is characterized by a pronounced sourness (not all varieties are as sour as San Francisco sourdough.)

The taste in San Francisco sourdough is so dominant a strain that it starter was named *Lactobacillus sanfranciscensis.*

It was in 1849 that the Boudin family struck culinary gold in San Francisco. They blame their luck on the San Francisco atmosphere. On their web site they explain.

> *Wild yeasts in the San Francisco air imparted a unique tang to their traditional French bread, giving rise to 'San Francisco sourdough French bread'. Today, the Boudin family's initial recipe lives on in the hands and hearts of our expert bakers, with a portion of the original mother dough still starting each and every sourdough loaf we make.*

There are many breads in which techniques similar to that use in making sourdough bread. For instance, baking soda (and sometimes baking powder) is added to a sourdough-type starter.

This neutralizes the acid in the starter and generates carbon dioxide in the process, providing a lift to the dough or batter similar in a manner to Irish soda bread.

In extreme cold, miners would put the starter ball under their clothes, next to their skin, or tuck it into their bedroll with them at night, anything to to keep the yeast in it alive.

Chapter 19

The Presidio

The Presidio served as a military reservation in 1776 as Spain's northernmost outpost of colonial power.

El Presidio Real de San Francisco (The Royal Fortress of Saint Francis) is now a park. The former military base is part of the Golden Gate National Recreation Area.

Congress voted to end the Presidio's status as an active military installation of the U.S. in 1989. The facility was transferred to the National Park Service, ending 219 years of military use.

The Presidio has many wooded areas and scenic vistas overlooking the Golden Gate Bridge.

Staff officers of the Pacific Military Division statopmed at the Presidio at the time of the San Francisco earthquake.

The Presidio was originally a Spanish Fort sited by Juan Bautista de Anza March 28, 1776. It was built later that year. The Presidio's original garrison was 33 men.

The fort was seized by the U.S. military in 1846 at the start of the Mexican American War. It became the base for several Army headquarters and units. The generals William Sherman, George Henry Thomas and John Pershing all headquartered there.

The Presidio was involved in most of America's military engagements in the Pacific. It was the assembly point for Army forces that invaded the Philippines in the Spanish-American War.

Beginning in the 1890s, the Presidio was home to the Letterman Army Medical Center. It provided medical care for thousands of the war-wounded during every conflict of the 20th Century.

The Presidio Trust now manages most of the park in partnership with the National Park Service. The Trust has jurisdiction over the interior 80 percent of the Presidio, including all of its historic structures.

Rents from commercial and residential tenants has given the Trust financial self-sufficiency.

Since the Spanish first arrived in 1776, the Presidio has had soldiers maintaining their guard over the riches of San Francisco Bay. The Presidio is the oldest continuously used military post in the U. S.

Before the arrival of the Europeans, Native Americans called the northern California region home for nearly 10,000 years. The Ohlone-Costanoan tribes seasonally occupied villages in what is now the San Francisco peninsula.

The Indians gathered shellfish along the Presidio's bayshore.

From 1776 to 1821, the Presidio was the Spanish empire's northernmost military outpost. It guarded California's largest harbor from being occupied by other European powers, including the Russians and Britain.

After an earthquake in 1812, the Presidio had to be rebuilt. At that time, its adobe quadrangle was doubled in size.

Presidio soldiers and their families spent most of their time farming and ranching at this distant outpost.

When Mexico declared its independence from Spain in 1821, it took a year for the news to reach *Alta California*. There was no change in personnel when the Presidio changed from Spanish to Mexican sovereignty.

Chapter 20

Tye Leung Schulze

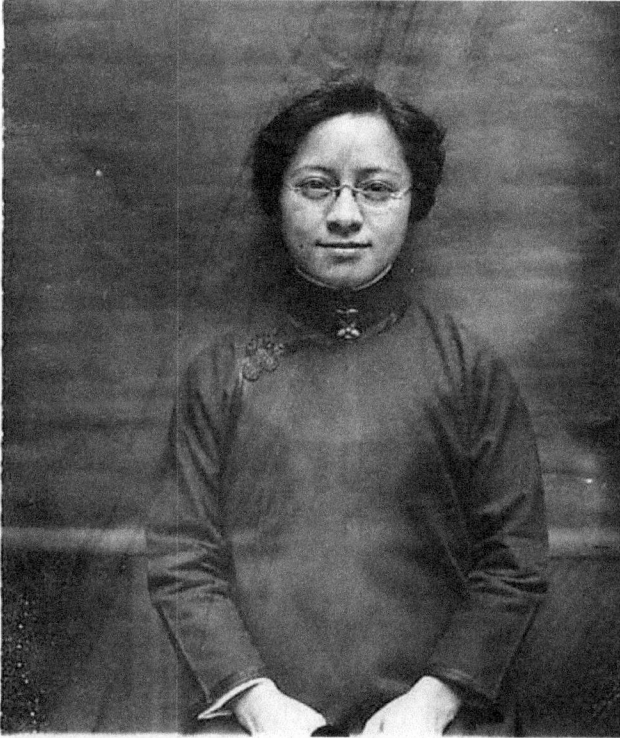

Tye Leung Schulze, at 25 years of age.

At age 12, Tye Leung Schulze ran away from home to escape an arranged marriage.

The youngest of eight children and the daughter of immigrants, Tye was born in San Francisco. Her parents came from the Guangdong province of Chinas.

Her father worked at a shoe factory and her mother ran a boarding house for women. Tye said she used to go to two gambling houses to get the leftover food for her family.

Tye was able to attend a missionary school to learn English. She was well-liked by her teachers and often attended church meetings with them.

When she was nine years old, Tye's mother sent her to work as a servant in another household. She recalled later that the family was nice to her, but she hadn't grasped that she had been sold to another family.

Tye's uncle learned of what happened. He took Tye to the Presbyterian Mission Home, run by Donaldina Cameron. Cameron arranged for Tye to return home.

When Tye was 12, her parents arranged a marriage for her 14-year-old sister. Her sister was to marry a man from Butte, Montana, whom she had never seen.

Her sister ran away from home with another man before the wedding.

Tye's parents then wanted Tye to take her sister's place and marry the same man. Tye, too, refused and ran away to the Presbyterian mission. The mission's director, Donaldina Cameron, became attached to Tye. She nicknamed her "Tiny" because she stood barely four-feet tall.

Tye served as an interpreter for girls in Chinatown who appeared in court. Her ability as an interpreter became so well-known that she was welcomed by every court in San Francisco and Oakland.

She became the first Chinese-American woman to pass the civil service examination and receive a civil service position.

When interviewed by the San Francisco Daily News about her experience as an interpreter, she said:

> *Dull? Never! I'm sitting there listening to my countrymen. I listen for little scraps about the great new movement over the sea, this setting them free over there as I have been set free here."*

Tye next got attention by being the first Chinese-American woman to vote in a U.S. primary election.

While working at Angel Island as an interpreter, Tye met and fell in love with Charles Frederick Schulze, an immigration inspector. Because of anti-miscegenation laws, they could not marry in California.

In 1913, the couple traveled to Vancouver, Washington, which allowed inter-racial marriages. Neither her nor his family approved of the marriage.

When they returned to San Francisco, they found their marriage had cost them their jobs. They found it difficult to find steady work.

Charles ended up working as a mechanic and telephone repairman for Southern Pacific Company. Tye worked for a year at the Chinese Tea Garden.

Tye then returned to school to learn bookkeeping. She got a job at the Chinese Hospital as an administrative clerk, bookkeeper and social worker.

Tye then worked as a telephone operator at the Pacific Telephone's China Exchange. This was a high profile job for a woman at the time and she stayed there for 20 years.

Her son Fred told an interviewer, "The thing I remember about my mom, she was always asked to interpret. GI brides, immigration, court cases. She never refused to help."

She and her husband had four children, two girls and two boys. Charles died in 1935.

In 1946, Tye was hired again by the Immigration office to work as an interpreter. The War Bride Act of 1945, temporarily lifted the ban on Asian immigration and allowed the wives of many Chinese men to join them.

There was a great need for interpreters and Tye worked at the Immigration Office for a year. Tye Leung Schultz died at age 84 in 1972.

Donaldina Cameron's work at the Presbyterian Mission Home in San Francisco continued to rescue young Chinese girls. Most of these women were brought to California as slaves. Some were as young as six years of age when the mission rescued them.

They were usually kidnapped, but just as frequently, they were sold by their parents in China, and forced to work as domestics and prostitutes in the United States. Donaldina is credited with saving more than three thousand women and children during her forty-seven years at the mission.

Slave dealers and brothel owners did not hold her in high esteem. To them she was *"White Devil"*.

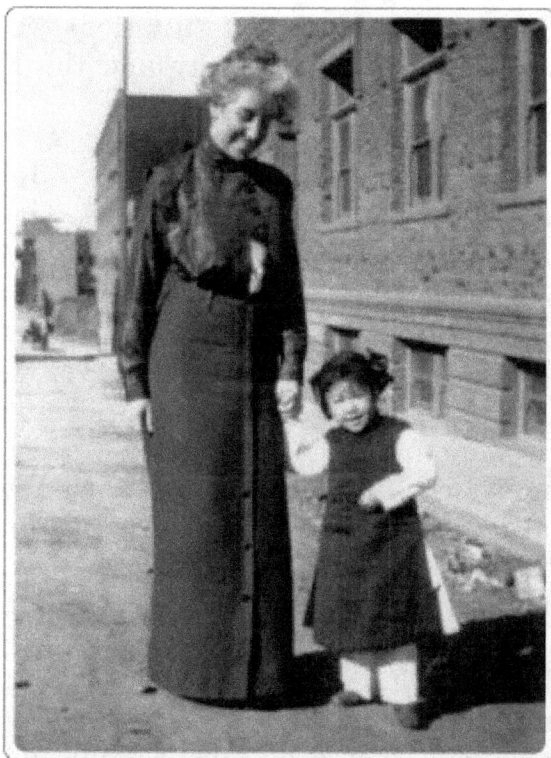

Donaldina Cameron was only 25 when she was made director of the San Francisco Presbyterian Mission.

Often the rescues consisted only of Donaldina and a companion. They would simply walk past the Chinese guards and escort the girls back to the mission. The guards were usually so confused and surprised at the sight of a white woman in the Chinese ghetto that they turned and ran.

Once safely in the mission, Donaldina and other missionaries helped give the girls a better life. They were taught English and reading and writing—according to their situations. The girls were introduced to Christianity and the Bible, as well as cooking, cleaning and sewing.

Many of the women were smuggled into the United States, circumventing immigration laws that excluded them. They were simply commodities that were bought and sold as property. The system was known as the *"yellow slave trade."*

Bogus contracts were created to keep the system working. The contracts were written with insurmountable conditions, making it impossible for the women to purchase their own freedom.

Some say the number of Asian women who died in enslaved conditions in San Francisco numbered in the thousands.

Gaining entry into the United States was complicated for the Chinese because of the Chinese Exclusion Acts of 1882, 1888, 1892, and 1902 and the Immigration Act of 1924.

These acts increased restrictions on Asian immigrants, especially laborers. Only students, teachers or merchants were admitted to America.

The acts were clearly discriminatory, as no other national group was denied entry to the country.

According to Paul Q. Chow, who wrote a thesis on the subject, the fear was that laborers from China would take jobs away from European-American workers. This fear was made worse because of the severe economic depression facing the country at that time.

When Donaldina Cameron, a New Zealand-born Scot, arrived in San Francisco from the San Joaquin Valley, her intention was to devote a "single year" working in the Chinese Presbyterian Mission at 920 Sacramento Street.

When she became aware of the slavery and conditions in Chinatown, she felt repulsed. From a mild-mannered missionary girl, Donaldina was transformed into a zealous social reformer. She became fanatically committed to wiping out the horrors of yellow slavery.

A San Francisco Examiner article by Michael Svanevik and Shirley Burgett detailed the lengths to which Cameron would go.

"Slavery was a fact of life in China," they wrote. "For centuries, young girls were taught to think of themselves as creatures almost purely for the enjoyment of men and were sold as merchandize to be wives, concubines or prostitutes."

Most of those arriving in California during the gold rush were sold for immoral purposes. State officials were bought off by the Chinese slavers and refused to recognize the existence of the slavery practice.

Most of the girls in San Francisco's Chinatown worked in cribs—narrow cells that accommodated two to six girls. They were required to service all comers, most of whom were white. Patrons paid twenty five to fifty cents for sexual services. Young boys were admitted for fifteen cents.

According to the San Francisco Examiner, The Presbyterian Mission spearheaded reform against the yellow slave trade as early as the 1870s. Margaret Culbertson, then the mission's director, instituted raids to liberate captive children.

Donaldina Cameron became Culbertson's assistant in 1895 and assumed the directorship two years later on Culbertson's death.

Cameron became the scourge of the underworld, the Examiner wrote. "She came to know every back alley and rooftop in Chinatown. She undertook rescues of young captives who requested assistance or when maltreatment of a child was reported.

When denied access to a crib or parlor, she relied on an unofficial alliance she had developed with San Francisco Police Sergeant Jack Manion, commander of the so-called Chinatown Squad. Manion sympathized with Cameron and ordered his men to "give her whatever she wants."

Police officers in plain clothes gained entry where Cameron could not. They simply pounded down doors with sledgehammers, crowbars and axes.

Plans for such raids were generally kept very secret, but word of them sometimes leaked out and the girls were herded into passageways, tunnels or secret rooms.

The San Francisco Examiner noted that Cameron did not limit her activities to San Francisco. She led raids in virtually every city on the Pacific Coast. She admitted that she often found it necessary to "break the letter though not the spirit of the law."

Not all girls came to the mission willingly. Many became so frightened at the appearance of

Cameron that they jeopardized their own rescues, the Examiner report said. At least some were forced into the mission against their will.

"The activities of Cameron and the Presbyterians endangered a very lucrative operation," the Examiner reporters explained. "Slave girls represented big money both for the brokers who imported them and for corrupt officials who looked the other way."

During the 1850s, girls sold for between $100 and $500. By the end of World War I, prices had risen to as high as $7,000. Yellow slavery flourished until the 1930s.

The slavery overlords expressed their displeasure with Cameron's crusade. On one occasion, a dynamite bomb was found on the steps of 920 Sacramento Street and disarmed without any damage.

Donaldina Cameron retired in 1938 after forty-seven years with the mission. Four years later, the mission was renamed the Cameron House in her honor. Donaldina Cameron died in 1968 at the age of ninety-eight

Chapter 21

Mary Ellen Pleasant

Mary Ellen Pleasant

Some called her the mother of civil rights. Others used uglier names. At birth, Mary Ellen Pleasant had no last name.

She said she was the illegitimate child of a Virginia governor's son (John H. Pleasants) and an enslaved Haitian Voodoo priestess. (As used in this context, the word "Voodoo" means spirit, and refers to the religion descended from a number of African cultures.)

While she won many of her frequent battles against inequities for others, Mary Ellen was never able to win the battle for her own good name.

At one time, Mary Ellen was the most talked-about woman in San Francisco. While other African-American women were seldom mentioned, Mary Ellen received full-page presentations in the press. Her story was about slavery, abolition, the Gold Rush, and the Civil War.

She covertly amassed a fortune once assessed at $30,000,000.

Mary Ellen was born a slave near Augusta, Georgia between 1814 and 1817. According to ship's records and confirming testimony, Mary Ellen arrived in San Francisco in 1852 to escape persecution under the Fugitive Slave Law of 1850.

As a child, she was sent to work in the service of a merchant in Nantucket, Massachusetts. She was a precocious child, and according to her final memoir, could recall the entire day's transactions in the general store where she clerked. This was indeed a feat, in that Mary Ellen could neither read nor write.

When her indenture ended in 1841, Mary Ellen married James W. Smith, a wealthy mulatto. While both Mary Ellen and her husband were mulattos, they each could pass as white.

The couple soon became allied with the Underground Railroad, helping slaves escape to freedom by various routes, but mainly on the railroad from Nova Scotia to Virginia (near Harper's Ferry).

James died suddenly. There were some who felt his death came at Mary Ellen's hand. Nevertheless, he left Mary Ellen a wealthy woman.

Pleasant continued her rescue work for the slaves by sneaking onto plantations. She became a much-hunted and infamous rescue worker. She fled to New Orleans to hide out with the family of her second husband.

In New Orleans, Mary had the opportunity to study with social-activist Voodoo Queen Mam'zelle, Marie LaVeaux. LaVeaux invented a way to use Voodoo to aid the disenfranchised, and Mary Ellen wanted to learn it.

The strategy she learned was how to use the secrets of the rich to get aid for the poor, a "model" that would serve her well in San Francisco.

Slavers continued on her trail, and Mary Ellen was forced to head west. She arrived in San Francisco April 7, 1852. The population at the time was about 40,000 people and to serve them there were 700 gambling establishments.

It was not a safe place, with five murders occurring every six days.

The California Fugitive Slave Act stipulated that anyone without freedom papers could be captured and returned to slavery. Mary Ellen took two identities to conceal the fact that she had no papers.

As Mrs. Ellen Smith, she worked as a white boardinghouse steward-cook. As Mrs. Pleasants, she continued her work to help her people escape from slavery.

Working as Mrs. Smith, she was able to get jobs and privileges for "colored" people in San Francisco.

She gained the nickname, "The Black City Hall." As Mrs. Pleasants, she used her money to help ex-slaves fight unfair laws and get lawyers or businesses in California.

Mary Ellen became an expert capitalist. Her own assets grew and she prospered. But when European emigrants began taking the menial jobs, anti-black sentiment and national depression mounted.

Mary Ellen owned boarding houses and many say brothels as well. She invested in mining operations. For forty years, her fortunes were tied to those of Thomas Bell, a Scotsman who amassed great wealth through banking, mining and brokerage.

Mrs. Pleasant built and furnished the 30-room Italianate mansion the Bells occupied with their six children and numerous servants at 1661 Octavia Street. She lived there with the Bells, running the household with an iron hand.

In 1891, she purchased a 985-acre spread in Glen Ellen that included the 150-acre Drummond vineyard and surrounding homesteads. She named her new property Beltane Ranch. It became a weekend home for her and the Bells.

Thomas Bell died in 1892 after falling over the stair balustrade in his Octavia Street home. The ensuing years found Mrs. Pleasant and the Bell heirs entangled in sensational lawsuits.

Mary Ellen Pleasant was declared an insolvent debtor in 1898. Her creditors alleged she deeded the ranch to Mrs. Bell in order to avoid paying her debts.

The following year, Mary Ellen's friendship with Teresa Bell came to an end. She was forced out of the house and ranch.

She died in 1904. At her request, her gravestone bears the epitaph "M.E.P. She was a friend of John Brown."

Chapter 22

Ansel Adams

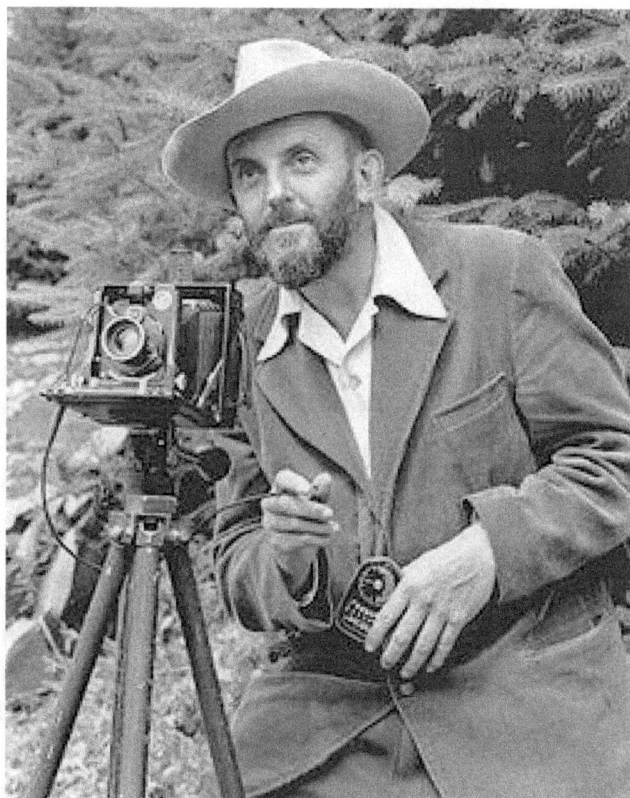

Ansel Adams

To say that Ansel Adams was the consummate photographer would amount to an understatement.

Adams was born in San Francisco in 1902 to Charles Hitchcock Adams and Olive Bray Adams. He was an only child and was named for his uncle Ansel Easton.

Ironically, his grandfather built a prosperous lumber business, which his father ran. Later in life, Ansel would condemn the very same industry for cutting down many of the great redwood forests.

During the 1906 earthquake, four-year-old Ansel was tossed face-first into a garden wall, breaking and scarring his nose. Although a doctor recommended his nose be reset once he reached adulthood, it remained crocked for the rest of his life.

Adams had little patience for games and sports. He took early to nature by collecting bugs and exploring Lobos Creek near his home.

Because of economic concerns, Ansel was pulled out of several private schools for his restlessness and inattention. His father pulled him out of school at age 12. He was then educated by private tutors, by his Aunt Mary and his father.

His Aunt Mary was a follower of Robert G. Ingersoll, a 19th century agnostic, abolitionist and women's suffrage advocate. His aunt's teachings and Ingersoll's influence weighed heavily in Adam's education.

During the Panama-Pacific International Exposition, Ansel's father insisted that his son spend part of each day studying the exhibits.

Adams visited Yosemite for the first time in 1916 at age 14. His father gave him his first camera, a Kodak Brownie box camera.

Adams and his friend Fred Archer developed the "Zone" system, which determines the best exposure and development.

He returned to Yosemite on his own the next year with better cameras and a tripod. In the winter, he learned basic darkroom techniques while working for a San Francisco photo finisher.

Ansel attended camera club meetings and went to photography and art exhibits. He explored the High Sierra, developing the stamina and skill to photograph at high elevations.

When he was 17 years old, Adams joined the Sierra Club. During the summer, he was hired as caretaker of the club's visitor center in Yosemite Valley. He was elected to the Sierra Club's board of directors in 1934 and served on its board for 37 years.

Ansel Adams photograph of Cathedral Peak in Yosemite.

Adams began selling his Yosemite photographs in 1921. His early photos showed careful composition and sensitivity to tonal balance.

Adams began experimenting with "soft-focus", etching, and other techniques. He used a variety of lenses to get different effects.

Between 1929 and 1942, Adam's work matured and he became more established. The 1930's were particularly productive and he expanded his works.

In 1931, through a friend, Adams was able to put on his first solo museum exhibition at the Smithsonian Institution. The exhibit featured 60 prints taken in the High Sierra.

"His photographs are like portraits of the giant peaks, which seem to be inhabited by mythical gods," wrote the Washington Post.

In the 1930s, Adams began using his photographs to further the cause of wilderness preservation. He detested the increasing devastation of Yosemite Valley by commercial development, including a pool hall, a bowling alley and a golf course.

Adams created a limited edition book in 1938, *Sierra Nevada: The John Muir Trail*. This book and his testimony before Congress played a vital role in the success of the preservation effort. Congress designated the area as a National Park in 1940.

In 1945, Adams was asked to form the first fine art photography department at the San Francisco Art Institute. He invited Dorothea Lange, Imogen Cunningham and Edward Weston to be guest lecturers. He asked Minor White to be lead instructor.

Minor White was a renowned teacher, critic, editor and curator. He was a homosexual at a time when homosexuality was strictly forbidden in this country. His sexuality was troubling to him. Nevertheless, he expressed it in his work.

Adam's legacy includes helping to elevate photography and art with painting and music.

We all know the tragedy of the dustbowls, the cruel unforgivable erosions of the soil, the depletion of fish and game, and the shrinking of the noble forests. And we know that such catastrophes shrivel the spirit of the people.

He told his students:

It is easy to take a photograph, but it is harder to make a masterpiece in photography than in any other medium.

In September 1983, Adams was confined to his bed for four weeks after leg surgery to remove a tumor. He died April 22, 1984 at age 82.

Chapter 23

Sam Brannan

Sam Brannan

Sam Brannan is the man that touched off the powder keg of "gold mania" that brought the world to California and other parts of the west. Brannan came west leading a party of 200 gold-hungry people from New York.

Brannan's arrival with the 200 potential gold miners immediately tripled the population of Yerba Buena (now called San Francisco).

By the time James Marshall discovered gold at Sutter's Mill, Brannan owned a newspaper, a hotel, a flour mill, and a store. He opened several more general stores, one of which was a store at Sutter's Fort. It was indeed part of Brannan's scheme, since he would profit by selling goods to the miners.

John Sutter and James Marshall wanted to keep the gold discovery a secret until Sutter finished construction of his sawmill.

Sam Brannan's store at Sutter's Fort.

Sutter offered his workmen double wages if they would keep the gold discovery a secret. He asked them to work on the saw mill during the week and look for gold on Sundays.

Brannan, editor of the California Star, a one-page San Francisco newspaper, had other plans after he heard of the gold discovery.

He was still in his 20s and soon was California's first millionaire. He shamelessly used the tithes of the Mormon Church for personal profit by investing in real estate and other ventures.

Brigham Young, head of the Mormon Church, dispatched an agent from Salt Lake City to recover "the Lord's money."

Brannan's reply to the messenger, "You go back and tell Brigham that I'll give up the Lord's money when he sends me a receipt signed by the Lord."

Soon after, Brannan was officially ousted from the church. He ignored the order of excommunication and continued to collect tithes to the church.

Several weeks after he learned of Marshall's discovery, Brannan bought everything in the region that might be useful to gold miners. He stored the goods in a warehouse near his store at Sutter's Fort.

Then, on May 12, 1848, Brannan appeared in the plaza at San Francisco waving a bottle of gold dust and shouting, "Gold! Gold! Gold from the American River."

People rushed to get gold mining supplies.

Historian H.H. Bancroft wrote of Brannan:

> *He probably did more for San Francisco and for other places than was effected by the combined efforts of scores of better men; and indeed, in many respects he was not a bad man, being as a rule straight-forward as well as shrewd in his dealings, as famous for his acts of charity and*

163

open-handed liberality as for enterprise, giving also frequent proofs of personal bravery.

When the gold rumors reached Monterey, they were not believed. On June 6, Walter Colton, *alcalde* or mayor of Monterey, sent a messenger to the American River to verify the gold discovery.

When the messenger came back with samples of gold, Colton said, "The blacksmith dropped his hammer, the carpenter his plane, the mason his trowel, the farmer his sickle, and they were all off to the mines.

Some went on horses, some on carts and some on crutches, and one even went on a litter.

"These gold mines," Colton moaned, are going to upset all the domestic arrangements of society."

Colonel Richard B. Mason could not prevent his soldiers from deserting, especially after one of them returned from a three-week furlough with a quantity of gold worth more than his army salary for five years.

It was a crazy scene in California. By the end of 1848 about four thousand men from various parts of California and about six thousand more from places like Hawaii, Oregon, Utah, Mexico, Peru and Chili were all at the California diggings.

Sam Brannan was taking in $150,000-a-month selling gold mining equipment and other supplies to the gold seekers. He no longer had need for the tithes he collected.

Vicente Perez Rosales, a Chilean gold miner, described Brannan's store at Sutter's Fort. "We saw there a cabin of unfinished boards, a few huts of woven branches and a short distance away a large store with a huge sign that read, 'Brannan and Company'."

By 1856, Brannan was said to have owned one fifth of the entire city of San Francisco and as much of Sacramento. He was said to be earning as much as $250,000 to $500,000 per year.

An affinity for whiskey and a bitter divorce settlement led to his financial ruin.

Chapter 24

Jacob Leese

Jacob Leese family

When the first emigrants arrived in California they found a thriving colony that included Jacob Leese.

Mexican laws governing the region made it difficult for aliens to enter or to live there. Mexican citizens generally winked at the laws and welcomed newcomers.

Take Joseph Chapman, for instance. Chapman was a crew member on a pirate ship that was captured at Monterey. Chapman married his captor's daughter, entered the boat building business and became a staunch member of the community.

In the late 1820s, a second wave of newcomers to Mexican soil came, not by sea but from the land side. These were the fur trappers who braved the snowy Sierra passes and settled down as carpenters, masons, coopers, silversmiths, soap makers, shipwrights and vintners.

Among these foot-loose men was Jacob Leese. Once an Ohio clerk, Leese crossed the Sierra in 1833. During that harrowing journey, Leese was forced to eat his favorite hound dog to stave off starvation.

He first established a partnership with two Monterey merchants, William S. Hinckley and Nathan Spear. The three men wanted to start a store in Yerba Buena.

Within three years, Leese was a well-established merchant in Yerba Buena, later to become San Francisco. He became the second established permanent settler on the peninsula. William A. Richardson was the first settler.

Leese owned the biggest house in the hamlet for which he paid $440 in merchandise. He wrote a friend, "I think it's a Dam Good Traid."

In his rambling structure, Leese staged the town's first Fourth of July celebration in 1836. The celebrants included 60 Americans, Britons and Mexicans who gathered at his large house.

Among the guests was Mexican General Mariano Guadalupe Vallejo. Mariano's pretty sister, Rosalia, captivated the host.

But General Vallejo had bestowed Rosalia's hand on an Irishman named Timothy Murphy, who was scratching out a living as an otter hunter.

The spirited tart-tongued Rosalia jilted Murphy and married Leese instead. As a side note, Murphy kept the ranch.

Leese and Rosalia had their first child, Rosalia, the eldest of seven, in 1838. Leese prospered for a time with such enterprises as a cattle drive to Oregon and making a trading trip to China.

Leese was thrown into prison by John Charles Fremont during the Bear Flag Revolt, for no other reason than that he was married to General Vallejo's sister.

He lost the lands he had acquired to hordes of squatters who poured into California in 1849.

He died, impoverished, after being run over by a wagon in San Francisco while walking home from an old timers get-together. He was 82.

Chapter 25

The Bohemian Club

The Bohemian Club

The Bohemian Club is a private gentleman's club. It was founded in 1872 from a regular meeting of journalists, artists and musicians.

In New York City and other American metropolises in the late 1850s, groups of young cultured journalists flourished as self-described "bohemians". The American Civil War broke them up and sent them out as war correspondents.

Bohemian became synonymous with newspaper writer. California journalist Bret Harte first wrote as "The Bohemian" in 1861.

Harte described San Francisco as the *Bohemia of the West*. Mark Twain called himself and poet Charles Warren Stoddard bohemians in 1867.

According to Michael Henry de Young, proprietor of the San Francisco Chronicle, the San Francisco club was initiated in one of the Chronicle's own offices. It was organized by members of the Chronicle staff.

"The boys wanted a place they could get together after work, and they took a room on Sacramento Street below Kearny. That was an unmixed blessing for the Chronicle because the boys would sometimes go there when they should have reported at the office."

When first organized, journalists were the regular members of the Bohemian Club. Artists and musicians were honorary members. The club then relaxed its rules, allowing people to join with little artistic talent, but who enjoyed the arts and had greater financial resources than did the journalists.

The club's motto is "Weaving Spiders Come Not Here," a line adopted from Shakespeare's *Midsummer Night's Dream*. The motto implies that outside concerns and business deals are to be left outside.

There's no shortage of famous names that have appeared at the Bohemian's shindigs. Donald Rumsfeld, Henry Kissinger, George H. Bush and Richard Nixon are a few.

The club has evolved into an association of rich and powerful men, mostly of this country. The membership list has included every Republican U.S. president (as well as a number of Democrats) since 1923.

The Bohemian Grove is the site of a two-week retreat every July.

While business is not supposed to be conducted at the grove gathering, it is said that The Manhattan Project, which produced the first atomic bombs, was conceived at the Grove in 1942.

174

Chapter 26

Lord George Gordon

Lord George Gordon was indeed a dapper promoter. He could con the feathers from a rooster. He dressed with impeccable taste, spoke with an English accent, and considered himself something of a Beau Brummell of the Western world.

Some said he was not a lord at all, and even questioned his British birth and English accent. Others were more unkind, suggesting he was born in New York's Bowery.

Gordon's first American adventure was to charter a ship to bring gold seekers from the east coast around the horn to San Francisco.

He signed up two hundred gold-hungry recruits for the trip, telling them they would sail in luxury from New York to California for the easy sum of one hundred and sixty dollars.

His only profit, he assured them, would not be made by the passenger fares, but by taking twenty percent of the gold that each of the voyagers took from the California hills.

Gordon's luxury sailing vessel turned out to be a wreck of a ship with no sleeping accommodations and little food.

While the passengers were crowded into quarters without bunks, Lord George was traveling overland with more than thirty thousand dollars the gold seekers paid him for fare. There are no records indicating the vessel ever arrived at San Francisco.

This didn't end Lord George's escapades. Once in San Francisco, he set about planning more elaborate schemes.

San Francisco was a disappointment to Gordon. Gold Rush San Francisco was filthy with a vast accumulation of ramshackle, temporary structures. Even so, Gordon recognized the city's possibilities.

Lord George proposed to banker Harry Meiggs that he and his friends give Gordon enough money to terrace Telegraph Hill and turn it into another Italian Riviera. There would be trees, shaded walks, monuments, and fountains.

Mr. Meiggs was not so easily taken in as the gold seekers. He informed Gordon, in no uncertain terms, that he, personally, didn't give a continental damn about beautifying the city. He only wanted to make money.

Lord George was not to be deterred. He suggested exactly how Mr. Meiggs could make money. They could build a great wharf where the waters flowing through the Golden Gate joined the waters of San Francisco Bay. The wharf, incidentally, would be called Meigg's Wharf.

This, Mr. Meiggs thought, did have a happy ring to it. And the fact that Meigg's Wharf would be the first name to greet incoming travelers interested the banker even more.

Lord George Gordon built Meigg's Wharf with a tidy profit for himself. History records that Meiggs, himself, turned out to be a thief who absconded

176

with funds belonging to several San Francisco widows and orphans.

Lord George had a miserable home life, having gotten entangled in a marriage to an alcoholic barmaid while still a young man in England. To escape this situation, he plunged into other ventures.

He started importing and refining sugar. Gordon built the first sugar refinery in northern California, making a considerable fortune. This sugar refinery became the nucleus of the vast Spreckels empire, which purchased Gordon's interests.

George was not done with his promotional talents, however. He envisioned developing some of the large acreage standing idle on the Peninsula, where William D.S. Howard and others had acquired great land grants from Mexico.

Lord George just knew the Peninsula could be transformed into the fashion center of the west. He purchased a tract of land there and built a fine home.

This home later became the residence of Senator and Mrs. Leland Stanford. The great acres, which Gordon had purchased, became the site of Stanford University.

Gordon never gave up on his idea of beautifying Telegraph Hill. Taking an architect with him, he walked across Market Street to the sand dunes at the edge of the bay. It was a dismal, windswept waste of sand.

"Isn't it beautiful?" George beamed to the aghast architect. "There lies the beauty spot of the

177

Western world—a gentleman's paradise! And we're going to build it."

When the architect responded that San Francisco needed a place for mud-grimed miners rather than a gentleman's paradise, George had a ready response.

"Mud-grimed miners become rich men. And rich men demand a paradise."

George described his plan. He would build a park at the base of Rincon Hill. There would be an oval garden with a high grille fence, much like London's residential parks. An artistic iron gate would stand at each corner of the park, and fashionable, London-style houses would surround the park.

Gordon's dream did become reality. Clipper ships came around the horn bearing English furniture and carpets to furnish the houses.

Men did make their fortunes in gold or in real estate property, and they came swarming with money in hand to South Park. The Hearsts, the Hall McAllisters, and others settled into the fashionable quarter.

The glory of South Park faded as warehouses and other industrial buildings were erected. Freight trains now rattle by it and above the site stand the stone piers of the Bay Bridge.

Even though Lord George accomplished many of his fanciful dreams, his dreadful family life drove him into a funk. Some say he died of a broken heart.

Meet the Author

Author Alton Pryor

Alton Pryor has published fifty-plus books since turning 70 in 1997—many of them about California's past and the colorful characters who rode our trails to fame or infamy.

To date he has sold more than 180,000-plus copies of his first book, "Little Known Tales in California History", and has done respectably well with most of his other titles.

But until fate derailed his 33-year journalism career, he never aspired to write a book, and certainly never anticipated he would come to be regarded as "Mr. Self-Publishing" by his peers in the Sacramento area. "I would have liked living in the Old West," he says. "I wanted, at one time, to be a really good cowboy. I had horses as a young man and even took a raw colt and trained it to work cattle."

But, by the time Pryor was born on March 19, 1927, the era of gunslingers and gold miners was over, and he started life, instead, on his family's farm outside of King City in the Salinas Valley.

He was terminated after writing for 27 years for a magazine. The magazine was sold to a mid-west firm. Pryor turned to writing books and says now, "I wish I had been fired 20 years earlier."

Index

182

183